THE EXPLANATION OF THE APOCALYPSE

AETERNA PRESS

PUBLISHED BY AETERNA PRESS.
COVER DESIGN BY AETERNA PRESS.

TRANSLATED BY THE REV. EDW. MARSHALL, M.A., F.S.A. FORMERLY FELLOW OF CORPUS CHRISTI COLL., OXFORD.

OXFORD AND LONDON: JAMES PARKER AND CO. 1878.

"BLESSED IS HE THAT READETH, AND THEY THAT HEAR THE WORDS OF THIS PROPHECY, AND KEEP THOSE THINGS WHICH ARE WRITTEN THEREIN."—APOC. 1:3.

"BLESSED IS HE THAT KEEPETH THE SAYINGS OF THE PROPHECY OF THIS BOOK."—APOC. 22:7.

ISBN-13: 978-1-78516-093-6

AVAILABLE AS AN E-BOOK:
WWW.AETERNAPRESS.COM

CONTENTS

PREFACE

THE Explanation of the Apocalypse by Ven. Beda is the earliest of the many works of our own writers on that Book, and, as such, may well deserve to appear in a form accessible to English readers. But independently of this, it is a commentary of much value and interest in itself, as is shewn by the constant use of it by Isaac Williams in his volume on the Apocalypse (The Apocalypse, with Notes and Reflections, Lond. 1852), and the notices of it in two recently-published Lectures of the Bishop of Lincoln (On the Millennium, Lond. 1875), who also, in his "Introduction to the Book of Revelation," terms it, "A valuable and interesting exposition" (Greek Testament, Gen. Ep. and Rev., p. 152, 1872).

The chief characteristics of Beda's method of exposition may be thus stated. The several visions are considered not to be successive, but contemporaneous, with occasional recapitulations, and to represent the condition of the Church in all ages, under different aspects. The thousand years, in the twentieth chapter, are interpreted of the present period of the Church's existence, in accordance with the opinion of St. Augustine, in the second part of his De Civitate Dei. The attention is closely directed to the text, and to corresponding passages of Holy Scripture, that the meaning of the symbolic language may be elicited. The previous exposition of Tichonius is mainly, but not exclusively followed. Beda appears, for example, to have adopted several opinions from St. Gregory the Great, and Primasius, as well as St. Augustine.

The date of the "Explanation" is circ. A.D. 710–716. It is described by Beda as an "Exposition" (see note p. 1). But it is called an "Explanation" in the printed editions of his works.

The translation is made from the edition of the Works of Beda by Dr. Giles, Lond. 1844, vol. xii., which, in this part at least, is merely a reprint of the earlier text. The notes are limited to the references required by the text, and the occasional notice of various readings, with some illustrations from other writers. Some additional notes will be found at the end.

For the sake of conciseness, the text, as read by Beda, which is not given completely even in the editions of the original Latin, where there frequently occurs the sign of omission, has not been translated in full. But the Commentary itself, by the addition of the usual numbering of the verses, and the insertion of catchwords in Clarendon type, has been rendered available for use with the original Greek, or with any translation. These words, though not necessarily so, are yet, by far the most frequently, from the Authorised Version. Care has been taken that the version may be as literal an one as is consistent with a proper rendering into English.

It may be stated, on information derived through the favour of Mr. E. A. Bond, that the MS. of the thirteenth century in the British Museum, No. 223 of the Harleian Collection, containing a Commentary on the Apocalypse, ascribed in the colophon to Beda, is a different work from that printed in Dr. Giles' edition.

EXPLANATION OF THE APOCALYPSE

LETTER OF BEDA TO EUSEBIUS

TO THE BELOVED BROTHER, EUSEBIUS, BEDA SENDS GREETING

THE Apocalypse of St. John, in which God was pleased to reveal by words and figures the wars and intestine tumults of the Church, seems to me, Brother Eusebius, to be divided into several sections

In the first of these, after a copious preface to strengthen the faith of the weak, and a description of, the sufferings of the Lord and of the glories which followed, he sees one like unto the Son of Man clothed with the Church, Who, after He has related what has happened, or is about to happen, in the seven Churches of Asia in particular, recounts the general conflicts and victories of the whole Church. And here, designedly, in the sixth place He has foretold that the Jews are to be made subject to the Church, and that there is to be a trial of the world at large, and that He Himself will come quickly; and He places in the seventh the lukewarm Laodicea. For "when the Son of Man cometh will He," dost thou think, "find the faith in the earth?"

Then in the second section, after that the four living creatures in the throne of God, and the twenty-four elders, have been described, he sees the Lamb, on the opening of the seven seals of the closed book, unfold the future conflicts and triumphs of the Church. And here, according to the custom of this book, he preserves the order unto the sixth number in the series; and then he passes by the seventh, recapitulates, and concludes the two narrations with the seventh. But the recapitulation is also itself to be understood according to its place, for sometimes he recapitulates from the commencement of suffering, sometimes from the middle period, and sometimes with a view to speak of the last affliction only, or a short time before. But this he observes as a fixed point, to recapitulate after the sixth.

Next, in the third section, under the likeness of seven angels sounding with a trumpet, he describes the various events of the Church.

In the fourth, under the figure of a woman bringing forth, and a dragon persecuting her, he reveals the toils and victories of the same Church, and assigns to both combatants their due rewards. And here the words and aetions of seven angels are also recorded, but not in the same manner as above. So in mystic wisdom he almost always retains this number, for neither in his gospel nor his epistles is the same John accustomed to say anything with remissness and brevity.

Then, in the fifth section, by seven angels he has overspread the earth with the seven last plagues.

In the sixth, he has manifested the condemnation of the great whore, that is, of the ungodly city.

In the seventh, he has shewn the ornament of the Lamb's wife, the holy Jerusalem, coming down out of heaven from God.

I have also thought that the seven rules of Tichonius, a man of the most learning among those of his sect, should be briefly enumerated, inasmuch as those who are desirous to learn, receive great assistance from them for understanding the Scriptures. The first of these is concerning the Lord and His body, when there is a transition from the Head to the body, or from the body to the Head, and yet no recession from one and the same person. For one person speaks, saying, "He set a chaplet upon me, as a bridegroom, and adorned me with an ornament as a bride;" and yet, certainly, it must be understood how much of this belongs to the Head, how much to the body; that is, how much to Christ, how much to the Church.

The second is concerning the twofold body of the Lord, or rather, concerning the true and simulated body of the Lord, as St. Augustine was better pleased that it should be termed. So the Church says, "I am dark and comely, as the tents of Kedar, and as the curtains of Solomon;" for she does not say, I was dark and am comely, but she has said that she is both, because of the fellowship in sacraments, and the commingling for a time of the good and bad fish within one net, seeing that the tents of Kedar belong to Ishmael, "for that he shall not be heir with the son of the free woman."

The third is concerning the promises and the law, which may otherwise be expressed as concerning the spirit and the letter, or concerning grace and the commandment. This appears to St. Augustine to be itself a great question, rather than a rule to be applied to the solution of questions. For it was through failing to understand this that the Pelagians either began, or increased their heresy.

The fourth is concerning species and genus. For species is a part, but genus the whole of which it is a part, as each state is a part of the whole province, and each province a part of the whole world. These terms, accordingly, have come to the knowledge of persons in general, so that even the unlearned understand what is enjoined in any imperial command. This takes place also in respect of men, as the things which are said of Solomon are out of proportion to him; and it is only when they are referred to Christ and the Church, of which He is part, that they become clear. Yet the species is not always exceeded, for such things are often said as more evidently agree with it also, or perhaps with it alone. But when there is a transition from the species to the genus, as if Scripture were still speaking of the species, there the attention of the reader ought to be on the watch.

He lays down a fifth rule, which he names concerning times, and it may, as appears to me, also be called concerning numbers. This he states to be of force, even in the case of legitimate numbers, by the figure synecdoche. For the figure synecdoche is either to infer the whole from a part, or a part from the whole. And by this manner of speaking is the question of the resurrection of Christ also solved. For unless the last part of the day on which He suffered is taken for the whole day, that is, with the addition of the past night too, and unless the night in the latter part of which He rose again is taken for a whole day, that is, with the addition of the dawning Lord's day, there cannot be the three days and three nights, in which He foretold that He should be in the heart of the earth. Now by legitimate numbers he means those which the divine Scripture more eminently commends, as the seventh, or tenth, or twelfth; by which, for the most part, either the whole course of time, or the perfection of anything is designated, as, "seven times in a day I sing praise unto Thee," is nothing else than, "His praise was ever in my mouth." And they are of the same value also when they are multiplied either by ten, as seventy and seven hundred, in which case, the seventy years of Jerusalem may be taken spiritually for all the time during which the Church is among aliens; or by themselves, as ten by ten are a hundred, and twelve by twelve are a hundred and forty-four, by which number the whole body of the saints is denoted in the Apocalypse.

The sixth rule Tichonius calls recapitulation. For some things are stated in the Scriptures as if they follow in the order of time, or are related in the succession of events, when, indeed, the narration is tacitly recalled to what has been omitted. As it is said in Genesis, "These are the sons of Noah, in their tribes and their tongues. By these are the isles of the nations upon the earth overspread;" and immediately, "But the whole earth was of one lip, and of the same speech." So it seems to be stated, as if at the very time when they were dispersed, they all had one language, when rather, by a recapitulation, he was secretly adding in what manner the tongues were divided.

His seventh rule is, concerning the devil and his body. For sometimes that is stated in respect of the devil which cannot be recognised in himself, but only in his body; as the Lord saith, among other things, to the blessed Job, in exposing the deceit and power of this enemy, "Will he make many prayers to thee, or will he speak soft things to thee?" And it is not the devil himself who is anywhere read of as repentant, but his body, which, when condemned at the last, will say, "Lord, Lord, open unto us."

So then, if any one will observe carefully, he will find these rules to prevail in all the canonical Scriptures, and especially in the prophetical parts, as well as in the Apocalypse, that is, the Revelation of St. John the Apostle, which the same Tichonius both understood with a lively apprehension, and expounded with truthfulness, and in a sufficiently Catholic sense, excepting only those places in which he endeavoured to defend the schism of his party, that is, the Donatists. For here he laments the persecutions which they endured from the religious Emperor Valentinian, as heretics, when their churches, and followers, and houses, and possessions were given up into the hands of the Catholics, and their priests were driven into exile; and he calls these things martyrdoms, and boasts that they were foretold in the same Apocalypse. Now we have followed on our part the sense of this author in the present work, but in so doing we have omitted some things beyond the purpose which he inserted, in order that we may be more compendious; and we have taken care to add many more, which to him, as a man of genius, and who flourished, as was said of him, like an open rose among thorns, appeared plain and unworthy of investigation; and this we have done, so far as we have been able to attain, either by the tradition of masters, or the recollection of reading, or even our own capacity; for this, too, is among the commandments which we have received, to return to the Lord with usury the talents which have been committed to us. Now, although it had seemed fit that the aforesaid work should be divided into three short books to relieve the mind; for in some way or other, as the blessed Augustine says, "The attention of the reader is refreshed by the termination of a book, as the toil of the traveller by resting at an inn;" nevertheless, that it might be rendered more easy for those who search to find, it was thought good that the continuous order of paragraphs should be preserved throughout, which I had previously noted in the book itself by prefixing marks. For, as I think that the indolence of our nation, I mean of the English, ought to be taken into account,—which too, not long since, that is, in the time of the blessed Pope Gregory, received the seed of faith, and has cultivated the same remissly enough, so far as reading is concerned,—I have arranged my plan, so as not only to elucidate the sense, but also to compress the sentences, inasmuch as brevity, if it is clear, is wont to be fixed in the memory more than prolix discussion.

I bid thee farewell in Christ, most beloved brother, and desire that thou mayest deign to be ever mindful of thy Beda.

EPIGRAM OF BEDA,

ON THE BLESSED JOHN AND HIS APOCALYPSE

AN exile from the busy haunts of men,
Forbidden now to see his country's soil,
He, loved of God, to heaven triumphant soars,
And joins the choir around the high-throned King.
His sacred eye the world below surveys,
As o'er its waters pass the fleeting ships.
Babel and Solyma in conflict join
Their several hosts. In quick succession here
They turn in flight, and here the strife renew.
The white-robed soldier of the gentle Lamb
May with his leader gain the realms of joy;
The scaly serpent in the dark abyss
O'erwhelms in hunger, flame, and pestilence,
His gathering bands. This warfare's dread array,
And art, and numbers, and its victories
Desirous to unfold, I've wandered through
The sacred plains, where those of old have sown,
Collecting thence some fruits. But few they are,
That no profusion cause to loathe the feast,
Nor e'en forbid the meaner guest to attempt
A preparation all too great. And now,
If these my scanty morsels please thy taste,
Give praise to God, Who reigns above the skies;
Or else, accept a friendly heart's intent,
And, armed with pumice, this my verse erase.

BOOK THE FIRST

ON CHAPTER 1

v. 1. The revelation of Jesus Christ. The progress with which the Church that had been founded by the Apostles was to be extended, or the end with which it was to be perfected, had need to be revealed, in order to strengthen the preachers of the faith against the opposition of the world. And John, in his own manner, refers the glory of the Son to the Father, and testifies that Jesus Christ has received from God.

shortly. That is, which are to happen to the Church in the present time.

signified. He wrapped up this revelation in mystical words, that it might not be manifested to all, and become lightly esteemed.

angel. For an angel appeared to John in the form of Christ, as will be seen more clearly in that which follows.

John. That through John He might lay open to all His servants the things which he, by the privilege of a peculiar chastity, obtained above all others to behold.

2. testimony. That thou mayest not doubt of the person of John, he is the same who gave testimony to the eternal Word of God incarnate, according as he saw, saying, "Whose glory we saw, the glory as of the only-begotten of the Father."

3. Blessed. Teachers and hearers are therefore blessed, because they who keep the Word of God find that a short time of labour is followed by everlasting joys.

4. seven. By these seven churches he writes to every church, for universality is wont to be denoted by the number seven, in that all the time of this age is evolved from seven days.

Grace. Grace he desires for us, and peace from God, the eternal Father, and from the sevenfold Spirit, and from Jesus Christ, Who gave testimony to the Father in His Incarnation. He names the Son in the third place, as he was to speak further of Him. He names Him also the last in order, as He is the first and the last; for He had already named Him in the Father by saying, "Who was to come."

5. the first-begotten. This is the same that the Apostle says, "We have seen Jesus Christ for the suffering of death crowned with glory and honour." And in another place, in setting forth the reproach of the cross, he added, "Wherefore also God highly exalted Him, and gave Him the Name which is above every name."

6. priests. Because the King of kings and heavenly Priest united us unto His own body by offering Himself for us, there is not one of the saints who has not spiritually the office of priesthood, in that he is a member of the eternal Priest

7. cometh. He Who was concealed, when at the first He came to be judged, will be manifested at the time when He shall come to judge. He mentions this, that the Church which is now oppressed by enemies, but is then to reign with Christ, may be strengthened for the endurance of sufferings.

pierced. When they see Him as a Judge with power, in the same form in which they pierced Him as the least of all, they will mourn for themselves with a repentance that is too late.

Amen. By interposing an Amen, he confirms that without doubt that will happen, which, by the revelation of God, he knows most surely is to come to pass.

8. A and Ω. He is the beginning Whom no one precedes, the end Whom no one succeeds in His kingdom.

Who is. He had said this same thing of the Father, for God the Father came, as He also is to come, in the Son.

9. I John. He indicates the person, the place, and the reason of the vision; and he also testifies that he saw this in the spirit, lest he should be supposed to have been deluded by a fleshly apparition.

Patmos. It is a well-known story that John was banished to this island by the Emperor Domitian for the Gospel's sake, and it was fitly given him to penetrate the secrets of heaven, at a time when it was denied him to go beyond a certain spot on earth.

10. the Lord's day. He indicates also a fit time for a spiritual vision, for Scripture is wont to express the reason of things in terms, as, frequently, of the place, or the body, or the air, and in like manner, the time. The Angels, namely, visit Abraham at noon, Sodom in the evening; Adam after midday was afraid at the voice of the Lord, walking up and down; and Solomon received at night the wisdom which it was not to be his to retain.

heard. He is first admonished by a voice, that he may direct his attention to the vision.

11. seven churches. The Church of Christ was not at the time in these places alone, but all fulness is comprised in the number seven. Asia, which is interpreted elevation, denotes the proud exaltation of the world in which the Church is sojourning, and, as is the method of the divine mystery, the genus is contained in the species. For the Apostle Paul also writes to seven churches, but not to the same as St. John. And although these seven churches are a sevenfold figure of the whole Church, still the things which he blames, or praises, came to pass in them one by one.

12. turned. Here the figure of the Church is beautifully represented, as holding forth the light of divine love in the brightness of a chaste breast, according to that which the Lord saith, "Let your loins be girt, and your lamps burning." And he denotes its perfection within and without by the two parts of the number seven; and the individual members of it, consisting of the four qualities of the body, "love the Lord their God with all their heart, with all their soul, and with all their strength."

13. Son of Man. He means that he is like the Son of man when He had overcome death, and had ascended into heaven. For "Although we knew Christ after the flesh, yet henceforth know we Him no more." And it is well said, "in the midst," for "All," he says, "who are round about Him shall offer gifts."

garment. "Poderis," which is called in Latin, "tunica talaris," and is a sacerdotal vestment, shews the priesthood of Christ, by which He offered Himself for us, as a victim to the Father, upon the altar of the cross.

girdle. By the "paps" he here means the two Testaments, with which He feeds the body of the saints in communion with Himself. For the golden girdle is the choir of saints, which cleaves to the Lord in harmonious love, and embraces the Testaments, "keeping," as the Apostle says, "the unity of the Spirit in the bond of peace."

14. white. The antiquity and eternity of majesty are represented by whiteness on the head, to which all the chief ones adhere, as hairs, who, because of the sheep which are to be on the right hand are white, like wool, and because of the innumerable multitude of the white-robed and the elect, who come forth from heaven, are glistering like snow.

eyes. The eyes of the Lord are preachers, who, with spiritual fire, bring light to the faithful, and to the unbelieving a consuming flame.

15. feet. By the "fiery feet" he means the Church of the last time, which is to be searched and proved by severe afflictions. For orichalcum is brass, which, by much fire and various ingredients, is brought to the colour of gold. Another translation, which renders it, "like orichalcum of Lebanon," signifies that in

Judæa, of which Lebanon is a mountain, the Church will be persecuted, and especially at the last. The temple also frequently received the name of Lebanon, as there is said to it, "Open, O Lebanon, thy gates, and let the fire devour thy cedars."

voice. The voice of confession, and preaching, and praise does not resound in Judæa alone, but among many peoples.

16. right hand. In the right hand of Christ is the spiritual Church. "On Thy right hand," he says, "stood the queen in a vesture of gold." And as it stands on His right hand, He saith, "Come, ye blessed of My Father, receive the kingdom."

mouth. He, the Judge of all things visible and invisible, "after He has killed, has power to cast into hell fire."

countenance. Such as the Lord appeared on the Mount, will He appear after the judgment to all the saints, for at the judgment the ungodly will behold Him Whom they pierced. But all this appearance of the Son of Man belongs also to the Church, for He Himself was made the Christ in the same nature with it, and He gives to it a sacerdotal dignity and a judicial power, and to "shine as the sun in the kingdom of His Father."

17. I fell. As a man, he trembles at the spiritual vision, but his human fear is banished by the clemency of the Lord.

the first. He is the first, because "by Him were all things made;" the last, because in Him are all things restored.

18. keys. Not only, He saith, have I conquered death by resurrection, but I have dominion also over death itself. And this He also bestowed upon the Church by breathing upon it the Holy Spirit, saying, "Whose sins ye remit, they are remitted unto them," and the rest.

19. Write. Reveal to all the things which thou alone hast seen, that is, the various labours of the Church, and that the evil are to be mingled in it with the good unto the end of the world.

20. stars. That is, the rulers of the Church. For the priest, as Malachi says, is "the angel of the Lord of hosts."

ON CHAPTER 2

v. 1. Ephesus. Part of this Church he blames, and part he praises, according to the character of the name. For Ephesus is said to be interpreted, "a great fall," as well as "my will in it."

stars. That is, Who has you in His right hand, and seeks you by His power.

walketh. Who goes about in the midst of you, and searches the hearts and the reins of all.

2. I know. I see, that is, that thou art diligent in the practice of good works, and bearest calmly the insufferable injuries of the wicked, for thou hast diligently examined the words and works of the false Apostles, and hast not been willing to give way to them in anything.

4. love. In the person of some, thou hast forsaken the love which began at first, and if they do not regain it, I will deprive them of the promised reward of light. But in others, thou hatest the examples of evil men, idolatry, that is, and fornication, for these are the deeds of the Nicolaitans, as is shewn in what follows.

7. ear. He indicates that he writes for all the churches the things which he addresses to them individually; for it was not the Church of the Ephesians alone, which, if it did not repent, was to be removed from its place; nor was Satan's seat at Pergamos alone, and not rather in every place. In like manner also, the other things of the several churches are common to every church.

overcometh. The "tree of life" is Christ, by the vision of Whom in the celestial paradise, and in the present body of the Church, holy souls are refreshed.

8. Smyrna. He speaks to this church of enduring persecution, and its name also agrees with this. For Smyrna is interpreted "myrrh," which denotes the mortification of the flesh.

the first. He who both created all things, and renewed all things by His death. This is a suitable preface when he is going to enjoin patience.

9. tribulation. Yea, "Blessed are the poor in spirit, for theirs is the kingdom of heaven." Fortunatus has beautifully expressed this in a short verse, saying:

"In narrow realm the poor man reigns possessing God."

Jews. "They profess that they know God, but in works they deny Him." For Jew is a name of religion. And so also the Apostle says, "who is a Jew inwardly, and circumcision is of the heart," "not in the letter."

10. devil. These words apply to the Universal Church, against which the devil is always exercising an enmity from which there is no escape.

ten days. He means the whole of the time during which the commandments of the decalogue are necessary. For as long as thou shalt follow the light of the divine word, thou must needs suffer imprisonment from the enemy who opposes thee. Some understand that the ten persecutions of the heathen, from the Emperor Nero to Domitian, are signified.

death. He shews how far the ten days reach, in that he counsels them to keep the faith unto death.

11. second death. He who shall have remained faithful unto the death of the flesh, will not fear the death of the soul.

12. Pergamos. Pergamos is interpreted, "dividing their horns," for by his judgment he made a distinction between the virtues of the faithful and the perfidy of the Nicolaitans, that "the horns of the sinners might be broken, and the horns of the righteous one exalted."

sword. He has fitly mentioned first His judicial power, for He was to assign rewards to the victors, and punishment to the transgressors.

13. seat. I approve indeed of thy patience, because although thou dwellest among the reprobate, thou dost not honour Me in name alone, as called Christian, but with perfect faith, even in the time of a persecution unto death. But I do not approve of this, that I see seducing teachers even in thee.

Antipas. Some understand a martyr who suffered at Pergamos, others the Lord Christ, who even now is put to death by the unbelieving, so far as in them lies.

14. eat. These are the two principal things in which all the carnal exercise themselves, "whose god is their belly, and their glory in their shame." But besides this, every evil work is idolatry and spiritual fornication.

15. Nicolaitans. The Nicolaitans are named from Nicolas the deacon, of whom Clement relates that, when he was reproved for his jealousy of a most beautiful wife, he answered that whoever would might take her to wife, and says that, on account of this, unbelievers taught that the Apostles allowed to all a promiscuous and common intercourse with women. And the Nicolaitans are reported to have put forth some fabulous and almost heathen statements

concerning the beginning of the world, and not to have kept their meats separate from things offered to idols.

17. manna. He who shall have despised the allurements of the flesh in spite of the advice of hypocrites, will of right be satisfied with the sweetness of the invisible bread which comes down from heaven.

stone. That is, a body which is now made white by baptism, and is then refulgent with the glory of incorruption.

name. That we should be named, and should bc, sons of God.

knoweth. Because "he who says that he knows God, and does not keep His commandments, is a liar," for the hypocrite tastes not how sweet the Lord is.

18. Thyatira. Thyatira is translated, "for a sacrifice;" and the saints "present their bodies a living sacrifice."

eyes. He explains farther on what eyes of flame are, saying, "I am He Who searcheth the reins and the hearts, and I will give to every one of you according to your works."

feet. This also he explains to be, that "the last works of this church are more than the first."

20. Jezebel. In thy work indeed, and thy faith, thou art to be praised. But in this thou art to be blamed, that thou dost not confute with proper energy the synagogue of false Apostles, which pretends to be Christian. The name Jezebel, which implies "an issue of blood," belongs to heretics; and in particular, she is conjectured to be a woman in the aforenamed church, who teaches the evil deeds which have been mentioned, who was to be a figure of the Jezebel throughout the world, whom also he manifestly threatens with vengeance.

seduce. Under the name of Christ forsooth, she taught spiritual fornication and idolatry, for how could she openly teach the worship of idols, when she said that she was a prophetess in the Church.

22. bed. It is brought to pass by the just judgment of God, that she should lie in a lied of eternal punishment, who made the wretched lie down in a bed of lust.

23. children. He here names the posterity and works of the woman, "children," and he threatens them not with the momentary death of the body, but the eternal death of the soul.

hearts. Under the reins he signifies delights, under the heart thoughts.

works. Our works and words, no doubt, may be known to men. But with what intention they are accomplished, and whereunto we desire to attain by their means, He alone knows Who perceives what each one thinks, and in what he takes delight. And with what consistency in punishing fornication and idolatry, which are open faults, can He be said to be a discerner of secret things, unless these names may be applied even to the least offences? "Thou wilt destroy," he says, "all those who commit fornication from Thee." And the same Apostle John, who heard this, when he reasoned of false brethren, ended by saying, "Little children, keep yourselves from idols."

24. you. As he commends repentance to the ungodly, and threatens them with punishment, so he exhorts the godly to patience by holding forth eternal rewards.

known. So, again, they who work iniquity know not God, although they preach Him. In this way also, God Who knoweth all men, knoweth not those who work iniquity.

send. I will not suffer you to be tempted above that which ye are able to endure; otherwise: "Beware," He says, "of false prophets," for I send unto you no new doctrine; but keep that which ye have received unto the end.

25. overcometh. The Church has this power in Christ, as the body in the Lord: for "in Him," according to the Apostle, "God has given unto us all things."

27. iron. With inflexible justice He rules the meek, that they may the more bring forth fruit, but overthrows the contumacious, that they may either perish for ever, or that earthly desires may be destroyed in them, and the impure things of the old man, whatever has been contracted and wrought in them from the sinful clay.

28. star. Christ is "the morning star," Who promises and reveals to the saints the eternal light of life, when the night of the world is past.

ON CHAPTER 3

1. Sardis. He reproves this angel, that is, the bishop, as not sufficiently diligent in correcting the bad. He commends him, however, as having some who walk in white, and the name Sardis agrees with these, as that of a precious stone.

name. To thyself, indeed, thou seemest to be alive. But if thou art not watchful in the correction of the wicked, thou wilt henceforth be numbered among the dead.

2. works. If a ruler has not striven to incite others as well, although he may appear guiltless before men, his works are not perfect before God.

3. thief. Here also, as in the parable of the Gospel, he warns us to be watchful by the example of taking precaution against a thief.

4. few. He said not a "few," but a "few names." For "He calleth His own sheep by name," Who knew Moses by name, and Who writes the names of His saints in heaven.

5. overcometh. He invites all men to imitate those who have kept the silken robe of baptism undefiled.

7. Philadelphia. Philadelphia is interpreted "brotherly love," and to it is the door of the kingdom opened, and the promise made of being beloved by the Lord.

key. That is, royal power, either because He was born of the family of David, or because the prophecy of David was made manifest by the dispensation of Christ.

openeth. The secrets of the divine law are opened to the faithful, and shut to the unbelieving, by the power of Christ alone.

8. door. By no man's power is the gate of heavenly knowledge, which Christ has opened to His Church, ever shut against it.

strength. He shews the reason on account of which the Church obtains these gifts, namely, that it does not trust in its own powers, but in the grace of Christ, the King. And it is the praise of God the protector, and of the devotion of the Church, that the gate of victory is opened to a little faith, and that a little power is strengthened by faith.

9. synagogue. He promises this to all the Church of that time, for it was not at Philadelphia alone that there were believers from the synagogue of the Jews, as we find in the Acts of the Apostles.

10. Kept. Because thou hast kept My example in suffering adversity, I also will keep thee from the impending afflictions, not, indeed, that thou mayest not be tempted, but that thou mayest not be overcome by adversity. And although the Church is always tried by adversity, yet, in this place, the hour of temptation, and the humiliation of the Jews in the time of antichrist, may be signified; that, as frequently happens in the course of this book at the sixth in order, so here also at the sixth angel, the last persecution may be designated. But as to this, it is believed that the wicked Jews will be deceived as well as deceive, but that others will understand the law spiritually through the instruction of the great prophet Elijah, and will be incorporated among the members of the Church, and bravely overcome the enemy.

11. hold fast. Do not grow weary in endurance, for I will help thee quickly, lest perhaps another, through thy failure, receive the reward which was decreed for thee. So it is impossible that the number of the saints which is fixed with God should be diminished by the faithlessness of the increasing tares. For if the lost crown is delivered to another, the place of him who has lost it is not vacant.

12. temple. He who has overcome adverse things for My sake shall be glorious in the temple of the Church, and shall no more fear any loss which adversity can bring. The pillars, that is, holy men, at one time strengthen the Church by their support, at another adorn it by their elevation, like the two pillars at the door of Solomon's temple.

Name. That is, because we are called "the sons of God" by adoption.

city. He shall be joined to the unity of the Church, which, by heavenly grace, is born again to a new life.

new name. This is the Christian name, not that it is new to the Son of God, Who had this glory before the world was made, but new to the Son of Man, Who died and rose again, and sitteth on the right hand of God.

14. Laodicea. Laodicea means "the lovely tribe of the Lord," or, "they were in vomiting." For there were there both those to whom He said, "I will spew thee out of My mouth," and those also to whom He said this, "Whom I love, I rebuke and chasten." But, according to the Greek, it is interpreted, "a just people."

Amen. Amen is interpreted, "truly," or "faithfully." Christ, therefore, Who in the essence of His divinity is truth, declared that, by the mystery of His Incarnation, He was made "the beginning of the creation of God," that He may train the Church by these things for the endurance of sufferings.

16. lukewarm. Thou art neither fervent in faith, nor entirely unbelieving. But, if thou wert still unbelieving, there would yet remain to thee the hope of conversion, whereas now, in that thou doest not the will of the Lord which thou knowest, thou shalt be cast forth from the bosom of My Church.

17. rich. Thou art content with faith alone, and it is in vain that thou layest claim to the treasures of righteousness. But if thou desirest to be truly rich, forsake all things, and buy the fervour of love, proved in the flame of afflictions, and anoint the eyes of thy mind, not with the antimony of deceitful boasting, but with the eye-salve of divine knowledge. To anoint the eyes with eye-salve is to gain an understanding of holy Scripture by the performance of a good work.

19. chasten. Do not shrink from suffering adversity, seeing that this is an especial proof that thou art loved by the Lord.

repent. He shews that there had been there such as were emulated and followed.

20. knock. I knock, indeed, at the door of thy heart with the right hand of exhortation, and if thou receive it willingly, thou shalt be deemed worthy of My dwelling with thee, and being fellow-heir with thee.

21. sit. By "sitting with Him" He means, being a partner in power and judgment "Who has made us sit together," he says, "in heavenly places in Christ."

overcame. The Lord, as a Conqueror, sat down with the Father on the throne, in that, after the conflict of His passion, after the victory of His resurrection, He manifested Himself more clearly to all, as coequal with the Father in power. Observe, that in all the churches the Lord first declares His own power, then recounts the works of the Church as worthy either of praise or blame, but always with admonition intermixed, and that in the last place He assigns to either part the reward which is due, and which may be understood both of the present and the future. But when He subjoins, "Who hath ears, let him hear;" we are without doubt to understand the ears of the heart for obedience to the commands.

ON CHAPTER 4

1. door. After describing the works of the Church and its future condition, he recapitulates from the birth of Christ, with an intention to repeat the same things in a different manner, for in this book he repeats under various figures the whole period of the Church's history. "Behold," he says, "a door opened in heaven." He fitly sees a door in heaven, as he is about to ascend, for that it is promised that the heavenly mysteries are to be opened to him, or, because Christ is the door. He who believes that He was born, and suffered, mounts up to heaven, that is, the light of the Church, and so is made spiritual, and beholds the things which shall be, as he says.

voice. That is, it was like the former voice which had said "What thou seest, write in a book."

2. a throne. The Lord dwells within the Church, which is fixed in a heavenly abode. Pope Gregoryinterprets the throne of God in the vision of Micaiah of the angelic powers, "over whose minds presiding on high, He disposeth all things below."

3. jasper. The colour of the jasper signifies water, of the sard fire, and we know that judgment is represented by these two. For "as it was," He says, "in the days of Noah, so shall also the coming of the Son of Man be."

rainbow. The rainbow, which is caused by the rays of the sun shining upon the clouds, and which was first produced after the deluge for a sign of propitiation, denotes that the Church is protected by the intercession of the saints whom the Lord enlightens, and these are well compared with an emerald, a stone of a deep green. For as they wait with a more perfect faith for an inheritance that fadeth not away, so do they by their prayer more powerfully protect the rest.

4. seats. The same Church which because of its fellowship in faith he had seen on one throne, he beholds, as sprung by a twofold testament from patriarchs and Apostles, on twenty-four seats, and it is seated because of its judicial dignity in Christ. So all the members will sit and judge, but in one and by one

Head. For how will saints be able to sit in the judgment, while they are standing at the right hand of the Judge? The twenty-four elders may also be understood of those who, by their loud preaching of the gospel, complete the perfection of work, which is represented in the number six for four times six make twenty-four.

crowns. That is, clothed with good works, seeking with an unfailing recollection of the mind the joys which are above. For frequently, under the name of the head, the mind is wont to bc understood.

5. proceed. This is the same that Mark says, "But they went forth preaching everywhere, the Lord working with them, and confirming the word by signs following."

lamps. He means the one sevenfold Spirit, for "there is one Spirit," and to be sevenfold implies perfection and fulness. But when the Holy Spirit has been mentioned, there fitly follows the water of baptism. For in it the same Spirit is believed to be received.

6. glass. Because of our faith in the true baptism, this is compared to glass, in which nothing else appears on the outside than that which it has within. The grace of baptism is also represented by crystal, which is formed from water, congealed into a precious stone.

eyes. All the parts of the throne of God, that is, of the Church, are filled by the light of the gospel, with the knowledge of the past and of the future.

7. living creature. The living creatures are interpreted in various ways. But the blessed Augustine, to follow the order in this book, says, that Matthew is intended in the lion, in that he describes the ancestral line of regal dignity in Christ, Who also has conquered as the lion of the tribe of Judah, for "Judah is a lion's whelp;" and in his gospel, as a king, he is feared by a king, is worshipped by the Magi, in which also the king takes account of his servants, the king makes a marriage-feast for his son, and at the last the king separates the sheep from the goats;—that Luke is intended in the calf, which was the great victim under the Law, for that not only does his gospel at the commencement begin about the temple and the sacrifices, but it thus concludes, "and they were continually in the Temple praising and blessing God." But the face of a man, he says, signifies Mark, who says nothing of the regal, or of the sacerdotal power of the Lord, and only relates simply the actions of the man Christ; and the eagle is John, for with keen sight he beholds the nativity of the Word, as the risen Sun. The living creatures, again, at one time denote the Evangelists, at another the whole Church; for its fortitude is represented in the lion, its sacrificial offering in the calf, its humility in the man, and its sublimity in the flying eagle.

8. wings. They raise the Church on high by the perfection of their doctrine. For the number six is called perfect, because it is the first which is made complete by its several parts, in that one which is the sixth part of six, and two which are the third, and three which are the half, make up the number six. Otherwise: the six wings of the four living creatures, which are twenty-four in number, intimate as many books of the Old Testament, by which the authority of the Evangelists is supported, and their truth proved.

eyes. The holy Church observes itself with vigilance, both before God and before men. The Psalmist had beheld its eyes within, when he says, "All the glory of that daughter of kings is within;" and its eyes without, when he adds immediately, "clothed around with golden fringes in variety." Otherwise: whether thou shalt attend to the letter, or seek for. an allegory, in the Gospel thou wilt always find light. Another translation has: "Full of eyes before and behind;" because the light of the Gospel both illumines the dark sayings of the Law, and pours upon it the brightness of a new grace.

rest. The holy living creatures for all the time of the age proclaim the sole dominion of the Godhead, the omnipotence and eternity of the Holy Trinity. For there abides in the heavenly places the continual praise of the intelligent creation.

10. fall. When the living creatures utter the sound of praise, that is, when the Evangelists preach the dispensation of Christ, the whole Church, which is composed of rulers and people, for so much is signified by the number twelve being doubled, falls at once upon its face, and adores Him "Who liveth for ever and ever."

cast. They assign, that is, to God whatever power, whatever dignity they have, for that He created all things out of nothing.

ON CHAPTER 5

v. 1. book. This vision represents the mysteries of holy Scripture, as laid open to us through the Incarnation of the Lord. And its concordant unity contains, so to say, the Old Testament without, and the New within.

seals. That is, it was either covered by all the fulness of the hidden mysteries, or written as a roll by the direction of the sevenfold Spirit.

2. angel. He indicates the promulgation of the Law. For "many" prophets and wise men "desired to see the things which the Apostles saw;" and, "of this salvation," as Peter says, "the prophets inquired diligently, and searched." This is the book which is closed both to the learned and unlearned in Isaiah, but of which even there the opening is thus announced, "In that day the deaf shall hear the words of the book." And of this Ezekiel also says, "And I saw, and behold a hand was sent unto me, in which was the roll of a book, and He opened it before me, and it was written within and without;" when he also added that which John concealed, namely, that which was written in the book, saying, "And there was written therein lamentations, and a dirge, and woe." For the whole course of the Old and New Testament forewarns, that sins are to be repented of, the kingdom of heaven to be sought, and the wailings of hell to be escaped.

3. able. Neither an angel, nor any one of the just, although delivered from the bond of the flesh, was able to reveal, nor to search into the mysteries of the divine law, nor to look into the book, that is, to contemplate the brightness of the grace of the New Testament, even as the children of Israel could not look upon the face of the lawgiver of the Old Testament, which contains the New.

4. wept. He was grieved, as recognising the common misery of the human race.

5. Weep not. He is forbidden to weep, because even then had been fulfilled in the Passion of Christ the mystery which long lay hidden, when, as He yielded up His spirit, the veil of the temple was rent For to Him it is said, "Judah is a lion's whelp: to the prey, my son, thou art gone up: resting, thou

couchedst as a lion, and as a lioness; who shall raise him up?" He proceeds to describe how, and when, the Lion of the tribe of Judah prevailed.

6. a Lamb. The same Lord, Who is a Lamb in dying innocently, became also a Lion in boldly conquering death. Tichonius says that the Lamb is the Church, which has received all power in Christ.

seven. The sevenfold Spirit in Christ is compared with horns, because of the excellency of power; and with eyes, because of the illumination of grace.

7. took. The Son of Man is said to have taken the book from the right hand of God, namely, the economy of the Incarnation, appointed by the Father and by Himself, in that He is God; because both dwell with the Holy Spirit upon the throne. For Christ, Who in His humanity is a Lamb, is also in His deity the right hand of the Father.

8. opened. For that the Lord, by His Passion, proved that the announcements of both Testaments were fulfilled in Himself, the Church gives thanks, and offers herself to suffering, that, as the Apostle says, "She may fill up that which is wanting of the sufferings of Christ in her flesh." For by "harps," in which strings are stretched on wood, are represented bodies prepared to die, and by "bowls" hearts expanded in breadth of love.

9. sang. They laud the sacraments of the New Testament, which are complete in Christ, while they extol with praise that same dispensation of it which they confess to belong to Christ alone.

redeemed. Here is further declared, that the living creatures and the elders are the Church, which is redeemed by the blood of Christ, and gathered out of the nations. For he shews in what heaven they are by saying, "And they shall reign upon the earth."

11. voice. Countless thousands of the peoples flow together unto the Church, and praise God.

13. in heaven. If the just are called "the sons of God," why not also the angels? But again, the heavenly host may also unite in singing that song, by rejoicing with us upon our redemption, as the holy Pope Gregory also has expounded it, saying, "For the voice of angels in praise of the Creator is the very admiration itself of inmost contemplation."

14. Amen. When the people within the Church make the praise of the Lord resound, the teachers confirm the same, and for example's sake, together with them adore the Lord.

ON CHAPTER 6

v. 1. opened. Seeing that the seals are first loosed, and the book is then opened, he has purposely changed the accustomed order. For in that He suffered and rose again, the Lord taught the Church that He was the end of the law; and in that He ascended into heaven, by the mission of the Holy Spirit, He strengthened the Church with the gift of a more hidden mystery. So He then opened the book, and now He looses the seals of it. In the first seal, accordingly, he beholds the glory of the primitive Church, in the following three the threefold war against it, in the fifth the glory of those who triumph in this war, in the sixth the things which are to come in the time of Antichrist, and that with a brief recapitulation of former events, in the seventh the beginning of eternal rest.

Come. We also are admonished by the loud voice of the Gospel to behold the glory of the Lord.

white. The Lord presides over the Church, which is made whiter than snow by grace, and He bears the arms of spiritual teaching against the ungodly; and in the persons of His own He receives, as conqueror, a crown; as it is said of Him, "He received gifts in men." In their persons also, although Lord of heaven, He was persecuted by Saul.

3. second. He is wisely bidden to observe the opposing horsemen, that, as he derives joy from the prosperity of the Church, so he may acquire caution also from its adversity, by foreknowledge of it.

4. red. Against the Church victorious and conquering there went out a red horse, that is, a malignant people, bloody from its rider, the devil. Yet we have read in Zechariah of the red horse of the Lord. But the former one is red with his own blood, this with the blood of others.

earth. That is, its own peace. But the Church has received an eternal peace, which has been left to it by Christ.

sword. That is, either against those whom he makes betrayers of the faith, or whom he makes martyrs. And concerning this it is said to the blessed Job,

"He who made him has made His sword to approach;" that is, either that he may not try the saints, as much as the ungodly one wills, or, that the vengeance of his own rage may return upon himself.

5. black. The black horse is the band of false brethren who have the balance of a right profession, but hurt their fellows through works of darkness. For when it is said in the midst of the living creatures, "hurt not," it is shewn that one is there who hurts. Of the running forward of this horse, the Apostle says, "Without were fightings, within were fears."

6. hurt. Beware, he says, lest, by your most evil example, ye offend your brother for whom Christ died, and who bears the seal of the sacred blood, and of the chrism. For whether they are perfect in merits, or are even the least, yet whosoever in the Church are imbued with the faith of the Holy Trinity, are redeemed by the same perfect price of the Lord's blood. And not without reason is the perfection of faith, or work, expressed by a measure of two pounds, and not by a single pound. For both alike have their root in a twofold love.

8. pale. Heretics who assume the garb of Catholics, are worthy to have death abide in their midst, and they draw after them the army of the lost. For the devil and his servants are, by a metonymy, called death and hell. It may also be taken simply, that there eternal punishment follows those who here are spiritually dead.

four (the fourth part). Behold the madness of Arius, which arose from Alexandria, and reached as far as the Gallic ocean, and pursued the godly, not only with a famine of the word of God, but also as wild beasts, with a material sword. Another version has translated it, "the fourth part," because the three evil horses, confident in their rider, the devil, attack the fourth, the horsemen of the Church.

9. fifth. Because he had said that the Church was afflicted in manifold ways in the present time, he speaks also of the glory of souls after the punishment of the body. "I saw them," he says, "under the altar," that is, in the secret place of eternal praise. For the altar, which is of gold, and is placed within, and near the ark of the Lord's body, does not, as the altar which is without, present flesh and blood to the Lord, but only the incense of praise; and they who now "offer their bodies a living sacrifice," when the bonds of the flesh are broken, thus offer to Him the sacrifice of praise. It may also be by transposition that he did not see them under the altar, but those who had been slain under the altar, namely, under the testimony to the name of Christ, as it is said also of the Maccabees, "They fell under the covenant of God."

10. voice. The great cry of the souls is their great desire for those things which they know that the Lord wills to do. For it is not right to suppose, that they wish for anything against the good pleasure of God, when their desires are dependent upon His will.

How long? They ask not this in hatred of their enemies, for whom they made supplication in this age. But in a love of justice, in which, as they who are placed near the Judge Himself, they agree with Him, they pray for the coming of the day of judgment, in which the reign of sin may be destroyed, and the resurrection of their lifeless bodies may come. For we also, in the present time, when we are commanded to pray for our enemies, say nevertheless, when we pray to the Lord, "Thy kingdom come."

11. robes. The souls of the saints which rejoice in their blessed immortality, have now each one robe. But when their bodies arise, as Isaiah says, "they will possess double in their own land."

rest. The desire of resurrection is not denied, but deferred, that the brethren may be gathered in and multiplied. For the joy of souls itself may also be represented by white robes, when they learn by the revelation of the Lord, that the ungodly are to be condemned at the last, and that even unto the end of the age many are to be joined to their number by martyrdom. Therefore, imbued with internal charity, and content with this consolation, they have been willing rather that their own joys should be deferred for the completion of the number of the faithful.

12. sixth. By the opening of the sixth seal the last persecution is announced, and that the world is shaken with darkness and fear, as when the Lord was crucified on the sixth day of the week.

sun. This is, as if the power of Christ were hidden, or His doctrine temporarily obscured, or covered by a veil, when the servants of Antichrist are brought to attack the servants of Christ.

moon. The Church, more than is wont, will shed her blood for Christ And he said "the whole," because the last earthquake will be in the whole world. But before that, as it is written, "there will be earthquakes through divers places."

13. stars. They who shine as heavenly ones in the Church, and that in appearance alone, when they are driven by the wind of the last persecution, will be proved to have been of earth. And their works are fitly compared to green figs, that is to the untimely, and useless, and falling fruit of the fig-tree.

14. heaven. As a scroll rolled up contains indeed mysteries within, while there is no appearance of them without, so will it be with the Church. At that time, known only to her own, she will prudently avoid persecution in retire-

ment, that by such concealment she may remain unperceived by those without.

mountain. He speaks of the members of the Church, as differing according to the character of their offices or powers, and foretells, that no one will be without his share in this whirlwind. But the movement caused by it will be dissimilar, for in the good it will be one of precaution by flight, but in the bad, of giving way by compliance.

15. kings. The "kings" we take to be those who are powerful. For he will have persons of every degree and condition to be understood. Besides, who will then be kings except the persecutor alone?

hid. While all the weak at that time seek to be strengthened by the examples of the highest in the Church, and to be fortified by their counsels, protected by their advice, and sheltered by their prayers, they entreat the very mountains to fall upon them with a feeling of compassion. For "the high mountains are a refuge for the hinds, and the rocks for the hedgehogs."

16. hide. That is, in order that He may not find us reprobates when He comes, but stedfast in the faith, with our sins covered by the intercession of the saints, and the mercy of God.

17. stand. He surely will be able to stand in that day who has now taken care to be watchful, to stand in the faith, to act manfully. But if thou refer this earthquake literally to the day of judgment itself, it is no marvel if the kings and princes of the earth are then afraid, and seek the refuge of the holy hills. For so, in the rich man clothed in purple, and the poor Lazarus, we read that it has already taken place.

ON CHAPTER 7

v. 1. four angels. That is, four principal kingdoms, namely, of the Assyrians, and Persians, and Greeks, and Romans. And as in the former seals, after the manifold conflicts of the Church, he saw the joys of triumphant souls, so now, also, he is to prove by examples the victory over the preceding kingdoms of the world, who have now submitted to the Church of Christ, which is to follow the reign of Antichrist. For greater matters must of necessity be confirmed by greater proofs.

winds. These, in a manner, stifled all things by their might, and suffered no one to breathe of his own free-will. In "the earth" is signified the variety of provinces, in "the sea" of islands, in "the trees" the different quality and condition of men. Otherwise: by the four angels are to be understood four winds, according to the prophecy of Daniel, who says, "Behold the four winds of heaven strove upon the great sea, and four beasts came up from the sea."

2. east. The Lord incarnate, Who is the Angel of the great counsel, that is, the Messenger of His Father's will, has visited us, "the day-spring from on high," bearing the ensign of the cross, with which to seal His own in their foreheads.

voice. The "loud voice of the Lord" is the cry which is lifted up on high, "Repent ye, for the kingdom of heaven is at hand."

3. Hurt not. From the time that the Lord suffered, not only was the dominion of the enemy who opposed Him destroyed, but that of worldly power too, as we both see with our eyes, and read of in the image which the stone from the mountain "broke in pieces."

foreheads. For to this end was the empire of the nations broken up, that the face of the saints might be freely marked with the seal of faith, which these had resisted. For, again, the figure of the cross itself represents the kingdom of the Lord extending everywhere, as the old saying proves:—

"Behold the world four-square, in parts distinct,
To shew the realm of faith possessing all."

And not in vain was the sacred Name of the Lord, of four letters, written on the forehead of the High Priest, inasmuch as this is the sign on the forehead of the faithful, of which it is also sung in; the Psalm "for the winefats," "O Lord, our Lord, how wonderful is Thy Name in all the earth?" and the rest, until he says, "That thou mayest destroy the enemy and the defender."

4. number. By this definite number is signified the innumerable multitude of the whole Church, which is descended from the patriarchs either by the lineage of nature, or the imitation of faith. For, he says, "if ye be Christ's, then are ye Abraham's seed." And it tends to additional completeness, that the twelve also should be multiplied by twelve, and brought to a sum of thousands, which is the cube of the number ten, by which is represented the enduring life of the Church. And for this reason, too, it is often denoted by the number twelve, because throughout the foursquare world it subsists by faith in the Holy Trinity, for three times four are ten and two. Finally, also, when the Apostles were to preach the same faith to the whole world, twelve were chosen, as signifying by their number the mystery of their work.

5. Judah. With good reason, he begins with Judah, from which tribe our Lord sprang; and has omitted Dan, from whom, as it is said, Antichrist is to be born; for it is written, "Let Dan become an adder in the way, a horned serpent in the path, biting the horse-hoofs, that his rider may fall." For he has not proposed to set forth the order of earthly generation, but according to the interpretation of the names the powers of the Church, which from present confession and praise is hastening to the right hand of eternal life. For this is the meaning of the name of Judah, who is placed first, and of Benjamin, who comes last So, then, Judah is placed first, who is interpreted "confession," or "praise;" for before the first step of confession no one reaches the height of good works, and unless we renounce evil deeds by confession, we are not fashioned in such as are good.

The second is Reuben, who is interpreted, "seeing the son." That works are denoted in "sons," the Psalmist testifies, when among the benedictions of the man who is blessed, he says with the rest, "Thy sons like olive-plants;" and below, "That thou mayest see thy sons' sons." For it is not, that he who fears the Lord cannot be blessed, unless he has begotten sons, and raised up grandsons, since a better reward awaits the faithful virgins; but in "sons," he designates works, and in "sons' sons" the fruits of works, namely, an eternal reward. Accordingly, after Judah there follows Reuben, that is, after the commencement of divine confession and praise, the perfection of action.

But because "we must through many tribulations enter into the kingdom of God," after Reuben follows Gad, who is interpreted "temptation," or, "girt."

For after the beginning of a good work, it is needful that a man should be proved by greater temptations, and be girt about for greater conflicts, that the strength of his faith may be approved. And so Solomon says, "My son, when thou comest to the service of God, stand in righteousness and fear, and prepare thy soul for temptation;" and the Psalmist also, "Thou hast girded me with strength unto the battle."

And because "we esteem them blessed who have maintained sufferance," for this reason, after Gad is placed Asher, that is, "the blessed," an order which is not unsuitable. For "Blessed is he who endures temptation, for when he has been proved, he will receive the crown of life." But, inasmuch as they who rely upon the sure promise of this blessedness, are not straitened, but "rejoicing in hope, patient in tribulation," sing with the author of the Psalm, "In tribulation Thou hast enlarged me," and also, "I ran in the way of Thy commandments, while Thou didst enlarge my heart;" and say, exultingly, with the mother of the blessed Samuel, "My heart is enlarged above mine enemies, because I rejoiced in Thy salvation;" therefore, Nepthali succeeds, that is, "enlargement." Moreover, he is followed by Manasseh, who is interpreted "forgetting," or, "necessity." And by the mystery of this name we are admonished, that being taught by the anguish of the present temptations, and "forgetting the things which are behind," we should so "reach forward," as the Apostle says, "to the things which are before," as "not to make provision for the flesh in lust," but as compelled by the necessity of human nature alone. And concerning this the Psalmist prayed, when sighing for better things, "Deliver me out of my necessities."

Next to him is placed Simeon, that is, "he heard of sorrow," or, "the name of his habitation;" in order that, by the character of this name also, he might more plainly inculcate both what it to be possessed here, and what is to be profitably expected. For the joy of the heavenly habitation will be given to those whose mind is here made sorrowful by a fruitful repentance; to whom it is also said, "Your sorrow shall be turned into joy."

In the next place follows Levi, that is, "added," in whom we either understand those who by temporal obtain eternal things; as Solomon says, "The ransom of a man's life are his riches;" or those who, by following the counsel of God, "receive in this world a hundredfold with tribulations, but in the world to come, eternal life." And to these, also, belongs this that is written, "He who adds knowledge, adds grief." For to this end also the bitterness of tribulation was added to the blessed Job, that having been proved, he might receive a greater recompense of reward. And so, not without reason, there succeeds him in direct order, Issachar, who is interpreted "reward," because, as the Apostle teaches, "The sufferings of this present time are not worthy to be compared with the future glory which shall be revealed in us," inasmuch as we fight with better success when there is hope of a sure reward. But God operates and perfects this in the habitation of strength, which Zabulon means, when "strength is made perfect in weakness." So that the body, which is considered weak by its enemies, and through the material substance of which they also strive to bring destruction to the soul, is found to be invincible through God Who strengthens it; and there succeeds a happy increase in this. This is also denoted by the word Joseph, for it signifies, gifts and graces to be added, whether thou understand the increase of spiritual gain from the double return of the talents, or whether thou take it in respect of the offerings which are made to God the Redeemer by the devotion of the faithful.

Now, in order that thou mayest perceive that all these, who both by the succession and interpretation of the names are shewn not to be placed without significance, will be at the right hand of Christ, the eternal King, in the judgment to come; Benjamin, that is, "the son of the right hand," is set last, as I said before, as the end of the line. For, after the last enemy, death, has been destroyed, the bliss of the eternal inheritance will be given to the elect. And this, whether each one of the faithful is rightly called the son of the right hand, or the whole assembly of the Church, of which it is sung: "Upon Thy right hand stood the queen, in a vesture of gold, clothed in variety."

So, then, from each tribe are sealed ten thousand. For in whatsoever virtues each one of the faithful has made progress, he must needs be ever strengthened by the faith, and instructed by the examples of the fathers of old. And it is most certain that frequently the body of doctors, frequently that of the whole Church, is designated by the number twelve, because of the sum of the Apostles, or patriarchs. For whether each one is counted worthy of praise from confession, as in Judah; or is illustrious from the progeny of works, in Reuben; or is strong from the discipline of temptations, in Gad; or is happy from victory in conflicts, in Asher; or is enlarged by abundant works of mercy, in Napthali; or is forgetful of the things which are behind, in Manasseh; or is still sorrowful, as in the valley of tears, but always rejoicing in the name of his habitation, while sighing for the heavenly Jerusalem, in Simeon; or is rejoicing together in the promises of the life that now is, and of that which is to come, resting upon temporal good things, added to the eternal good, in Levi; or is strengthened by the contemplation of the future reward, in Issachar; or is laying down his life for Christ, in Zabulon; or is labouring earnestly for an increase of spiritual substance, and offering something more beyond the commands of God, either in virginity, or from the abundance of his means, in

Joseph; or is expecting the right hand of eternal bliss, with unwearied prayer, in Benjamin; it is fitting that each should be sealed in his own profession by the rule of the preceding fathers, as by the number twelve, and that from the merits of individuals, should the most perfect beauty of the Church, as the sum of a hundred and forty-four thousand, be made up.

9. multitude. On the conclusion of the recapitulation, which had been interposed for the sake of example, he returns to the previous order, and announces the glory of those who are to overcome the wickedness of the last persecution. And that which follows, "From all nations, and tribes, and peoples, and tongues," may also be thus understood, that, after enumerating the tribes of Israel, to whom the Gospel was first preached, he desires to make mention of the salvation of the Gentiles as well.

robes. By "robes" he signifies baptism, by "palms" the triumph of the Cross, and he intimates that in Christ they have overcome the world. But robes may also double the glory which is given by the Holy Spirit.

10. cried. They proclaim with a loud voice, that is, with great devotion, an unceasing praise, that on the throne, namely, in the Church, there reign the Father and the Son; the Holy Spirit, nevertheless, reigning together with them. For it is said, "To Him Who sitteth upon the throne, and to the Lamb;" in the same manner as it is said in the Gospel, "And may know Thee, the true and only God, and Jesus Christ, Whom Thou hast sent;" in which place, "may know the only and true God" is understood.

11. angels. In all the angels he has represented the persons of the great multitude worshipping the Lord. "All they," he says, "who are round about Him will offer gifts."

fell. In this passage he relates, that neither the multitude, nor the living creatures, nor the elders worshipped, but the angels alone. For these are the multitude, these the living creatures and the elders. But it may also be understood of the angelic spirits themselves, of whom, as rejoicing together at the salvation of the Gentiles, it is said, "Rejoice, ye Gentiles, with His people," and, "Let all the angels of God worship Him."

12. blessing. The Church offers the sevenfold praise of excellence unto the Lord, and in each of its members confesses to have received this from Him.

13. who? He asks for this end, that he may teach.

14. tribulation. "Through many tribulations we must enter into the kingdom of God," but who knows not that the tribulation of Antichrist will be greater than all the rest?

washed. He speaks not of martyrs alone. They are washed in their own blood. But the blood of Jesus, the Son of God, cleanses the whole Church from all sin, therefore are they before the throne of God. For they are accounted worthy to stand there together in the service of God, who in the midst of adverse things are faithful confessors of His Name.

15. day and night. He speaks after out manner, and signifies eternity.

throne. The saints are the throne of God, above whom and among whom the Lord for ever dwells.

16. hunger. This it is which the Lord Himself promised, saying, "I am the bread of life: he who cometh to Me shall never hunger; and he who believeth in Me shall never thirst." Yea, "Blessed are they who hunger and thirst after righteousness, for they shall be filled."

the sun. "We passed," he says, "through fire and water, and thou broughtest us out into a place of refreshment."

17. the Lamb. He says, that the Lamb is in the midst of the throne, in that he had said above, that "the Lamb received the book from Him Who sitteth upon the throne;" and teaches that the Church is one throne for the Father and the Son, in which one God, the undivided Trinity, dwells through faith.

fountains. That is to say, to the company of the saints, who are the fountains of heavenly doctrine. The vision of God itself may also be signified, "in Whom are hidden the treasures of wisdom and knowledge;" according to this that David says, "As the hart longeth for the fountains of waters, so longeth my soul after Thee, O God."

tears. When the fulness of immortal bliss is gained, all sorrow will be at once consigned to forgetfulness. For, "Blessed are they who mourn, for they shall be comforted." The vision of the white-robed multitude may also be understood of the present time, when "we are saved in hope," and "hoping for that which we see not, in patience wait for it."

ON CHAPTER 8

v. 1. seal. It is believed that after the death of Antichrist, there will be some little rest in the Church, which Daniel thus foretold: "Blessed is he who waiteth and cometh to the one thousand three hundred and thirty-five days." And it is thus interpreted by the blessed Jerome: "Blessed," he says, "is he, who when Antichrist is slain, beyond the one thousand two hundred and ninety days, that is, three years and a half, waits for the forty-five days, in which the Lord and Saviour is to come in His own Majesty. Now for what reason, after the destruction of Antichrist, there is silence for forty-five days, is a subject of divine knowledge, unless perhaps we say, the deferring of the kingdom of the saints is the trial of patience." Observe that at the sixth seal, he sees the greatest afflictions of the Church, at the seventh, rest. For the Lord was crucified on the sixth day of the week, and rested on the Sabbath, awaiting the time of resurrection. Thus far concerning the opening of the closed book, and the six seals. But now he recapitulates from the beginning, as he is about to say the same things in another manner.

BOOK THE SECOND

2. trumpets. The Church, which is often presented under the number seven, is commended to the office of preaching. And here the first trumpet denotes the common destruction of the ungodly in the fire and hail; the second, the expulsion of the devil from the Church for the fiercer burning of the sea of the world; the third, the falling away of heretics from the Church, and their corruption of the streams of Holy Scripture; the fourth, the defection of false brethren in the darkening of the stars; the fifth, the greater hostility of heretics, the precursors of the time of Antichrist; the sixth, the open war of Antichrist and his own against the Church, and the destruction of the same enemy interposed by a recapitulation from the advent of the Lord; the seventh, the day of judgment, in which the Lord is to render to His own their reward, and to exterminate those who have corrupted the earth.

3. came He says not, came afterwards; but on announcing that the angels have received trumpets, he returns to explain in what manner they have received them. For although the Church preached before the coming of the Lord, it was not in every place, until it was strengthened by His Spirit.

stood before. stood before. He appeared, that is, in the sight of the Church, Himself made the censer from which God received the odour of a sweet savour, and was propitiated towards the world. Another version has, "upon the altar;" because on the altar of the cross, He offered to the Father for us His own golden censer, that is, His own immaculate body, conceived by the Holy Spirit.

incense. He offered incense from the prayers of the saints. For the Church entrusted to Him her prayers, saying, "Let my prayer be directed before Thee, as incense." The same is said both to have taken of the prayers of the saints and to have offered, because the prayers of all can come with a sweet savour to the Father by Him.

4. smoke. When Christ the Lord offered Himself a sacrifice of a sweet savour, the compunction of heart in the saints was made acceptable, for this arises from fire within, and like smoke is accustomed to excite tears.

5. censer. He fitly introduces a censer filled with fire, for "God giveth not the Spirit by measure." And this we know to have been specially fulfilled in respect of the Incarnation of Christ, "for in Him dwelleth all the fulness of the Godhead bodily."

earth. So also the Lord in the Gospel says, "I am come to send fire upon the earth.

earthquake. He shook the earth by the thunder of divine threatening, and the voice of exhortation, and the lightning of miracles, when some persecuted and some followed; when the latter said, "He is a good man," and the former, "Nay, but He deceiveth the people."

6. to sound. The Church, inflamed by the sevenfold Spirit, prepared herself to preach with confidence, so as to throw down the glory of the world like the walls of Jericho with heavenly trumpets. For that compassing about for seven days also suggests the whole time of the Church.

7. first. The announcement of the plagues is rightly compared to a trumpet, which is the signal of battle. For he saith, "Lift up thy voice as a trumpet, and declare unto My people their iniquities;" and in another place, "Let there be a trumpet in thy mouth, as an eagle upon the house of the Lord," that is, proclaim with a loud voice that Nebuchadnezzar will come for the destruction of the temple.

hail. That the punishment of hell is due to works of blood is announced by the voice of preachers, who say, "they shall pass from snow-water to excessive heat." The spiritual death of the soul may also be understood under the name of blood. Tichonius explains the verse in this way: "There followed the wrath of God, upon which the death of many should ensue."

burnt up. The life of the good is found in doctors and hearers. For, "Blessed," he says, "is he who reads, and he who hears the words of the prophecy." But the third part of the bad has neither of these. For, "the earth, which brings forth fruit in patience, receives blessing from the Lord; but the bad produces thorns and thistles, whose end is for burning." So also the Father, Who is the husbandman, cultivates the fruitful, but cuts down the barren tree, and delivers it as fuel to the fire.

grass. The grass is all flesh, which is now pampered with the softness of luxury, but which, when the sun of judgment is hot, loses the flower of beauty, and as the Lord says, "To-day is in the field, and to-morrow is cast into the oven." Tichonius speaks in this way of the third part in this place: "By the third he means intestine foes." But whatever is without the Church is called a third part, and the Church is a third which is to fight against a twofold evil.

8. mountain. As the Christian religion increased, the devil, swollen with pride and burning with the fire of his rage, was cast into the sea of the world, for that the Lord says, "If ye shall say unto this mountain, Be thou removed, and cast thyself into the sea, it shall be done." Not that he was not there before, but that when he was cast out from the Church, he began to rage with greater madness against his own, while through the pride of carnal knowledge he wrought in them spiritual death; for, "To be carnally minded is death." But flesh and blood taught not the Apostles, but the Father who is in heaven, for they directed the ship of faith in that sea, which yielded itself to be trodden by the feet of the Lord.

9. life. He said, "Which have lives," to represent the living, as spiritually dead; as the Apostle says of the widow who is living in pleasure, "she is dead, while she liveth."

were destroyed. Another version, by saying, "and they destroyed the third part of the ships," signifies that the third part which was dead killed another third, namely, that which came next to itself, by an injurious tradition, and following of unprofitable doctrine.

10. star. Heretics, who are called by the Apostle Jude, "stars of seduction," fall from the height of the Church, and by the flame of their own wickedness they endeavour to corrupt the fountains of the divine Scripture, not the sense of which alone, but also the words, they dare to falsify. These are worthy of the name of Wormwood, for a slight admixture of it is wont to make bitter much sweetness.

11. died. For "many," as the Apostle says, "follow their own luxuries, through whom the way of truth is evil spoken of." By the people of God, however, as Moses teaches, every kind of water can be drunk.

12. moon. The glory of the Church, which shines like a star, is often obscured through false brethren, who, either in the prosperity or adversity of the age, cause it to shine less brightly by their defection.

shone not. Another version has this, "And that the third part of the day might appear, and of the night likewise." That is, it was smitten for tins end, that the third part of the day and the third of the night might appear either to be Christ's or the devil's. To this end, I say, it was smitten, that is, was given up to its own desires, that as its sins became more abundant and more flagrant, it might in its own time be revealed.

13. eagle. The voice of this eagle daily flies through the mouths of eminent doctors in the Church, when they announce that the cruelty of Antichrist and the day of judgment will come with all severity to those who are lovers of the earth; while they say, "In the last days perilous times will be at hand, and men will be lovers of themselves;" and below, "men corrupt in mind, reprobate concerning the faith;" and in another place, "Then will the wicked one be revealed, who opposes and exalts himself above all that is called God, or is worshipped;" and again, "The day of the Lord will so come, as a thief in the night; for when they shall say, peace and security, then sudden destruction come upon them."

three. Not that the trumpets of the angels bring the plagues upon the world, but that each of them in his own time announces such as are coming, or are to come.

ON CHAPTER 9

v. 1. star. He declares with what fuel the flame of heretics, of which he had spoken briefly, was kindled. The old enemy forsooth, whom the Lord saw "like lightning fall from heaven," opened the heart of his own by blasphemous doctrine, and taught them to speak impiety against the Most High.

2. smoke. The madness of heresy rages to announce beforehand the great furnace, namely, the last persecution; and it labours to obscure not the weak alone, who like the air touch, as it were, the confines of earth and heaven, but the light also of the lofty, though unable to extinguish it For even the elect, if it be possible, will be led into error.

3. locusts. As the saints are the body of Christ and members one of another, so also the members of the flesh of the dragon cleave to one another, and are born one from the other, and the smoke of heretical blindness generates the pride of the ungodly, which hurts with its mouth. And although these are shaken by the wind of exaltation, yet they leave not the places of earth, for so also the smoke from which they are produced, though it seek to ascend, always sinks back into itself.

power. Heretics are compared with hostile powers, and appear harmless in their countenance, but keep poison in their hinder parts.

4. grass. He shews that the locusts are men, for they are not sent to the grass, but to men, for we understand locusts simply in this place.

seal. They are said to have the seal of God on their foreheads who have it, as they ought to have; and the number of these was reckoned above, as being inviolate and fixed by the angel, who brought from the east the seal of the living God. For here he has been pleased to use the form of speech in which it is said, "No man saith that Jesus is the Lord, but in the Holy Ghost," that is, perfectly and truly.

5. kill. Although heretics are supported by the secular power, and are permitted for a time to assail the good, yet, as the Lord saith, "they are not able to kill the soul." For by the five months he signifies the time of the age, because

of the division into five of the sense which we use in this life. But in that another translation has "six months," it agrees with this interpretation, because of the six periods of the age.

scorpion. As the scorpion diffuses poison from its hinder parts, so the ungodliness of the wicked injures from their hinder parts, when by threats or blandishments it causes the temporal things which are behind to be preferred to the eternal good things which are before. In opposition to the parable of the Gospel, the generation of vipers gives this scorpion to its own offspring.

6. death. They would rather that a life of misery should be ended by a speedy death, as the blessed Cyprian complained that it happened under the Decian persecution. "When they wished to the," he says, "it was not permitted them to be slain."

7. horses. That is, they are like the last persecutors. For in the last war which he is to describe under the next angel, he says that horses fight; or simply, as horses are urged to battle, not by any reason of their own, but by the impulse of the rider; so evil teachers, urged by a demoniacal spirit, attack the Church.

crowns. The twenty-four angels, who are the Church, have crowns of gold. But these have crowns like gold, as pretending to false triumphs from an empty victory.

faces. In the human face he represents a pretence of reason; in the hair of women, lax and effeminate manners; in the teeth of lions, which are wont to tear in pieces, and which bring with them a natural stench, ferocity of mind and the infamy of evil doctrine; and in breastplates of iron, hearts which are hardened against the truth. For "these having a form of godliness, but denying its power," "come in sheep's clothing, but inwardly are ravening wolves."

9. wings. It is matter for fear rather than exposition, that this army has its powers so greatly increased. First, the smoke ascends, then it produces locusts, which at first are compared to scorpions, and presently afterwards to horses and lions. Their power too would be great enough, even if they did not come armed with breastplates; but now they are said to be winged, and like chariots of war.

10. tails. As the scorpion goes along softly, but strikes with its tail, so the pernicious craftiness of the wicked seems in appearance gentle and harmless, but in that it secretly destroys as in some hidden manner, it brings with it death.

five months. Again he signifies this life, in which falsehood may avail either to catch the unprofitable, or torment for a time the spiritual.

11. king. God, supremely good, in His secret but just counsels, permitted an angel, not unfit for such as these, to have rule over them.

12. past. Since he had foretold that three woes were to come, he now mentions that one hath already come, in the deceit of heresy, and that two remain, which will happen to the perverse in the time of Antichrist, and at the day of judgment.

13. sixth. The sixth angel denotes the preachers of the last conflict, who, as the Gospel forewarns, detect the frauds of Antichrist. For the horns of the golden altar are the Gospels, which rise above the Church.

14. four. He signifies how much the Church will be persecuted at the end of the world, by the old enemy with his satellites, who from the time of the Lord's Passion is shut up in the hearts of the ungodly, and is restrained by the divine power from injuring it as much as he desires. For the Euphrates, which is a river of Babylon, signifies the power of the kingdom of the world, and the waves of persecutors. This is the great mountain, which he had foretold would be cast in burning fire into the sea.

15. loosed. In the same manner as prophecy, which points out to us things to come, he himself in spirit sees them come to pass. And he has said four angels, because the persecution will rage in the four parts of the world. For these are they whom he saw above, standing at the four corners of the earth, and restrained from injuring the earth and the sea for the sealing of the servants of God.

prepared. The malignant spirits, who at every moment of the hours and times hunger for the death of man, are then permitted for the trial of the Church to rage more freely, and are to be destroyed in their time? But what, thinkest thou, will they do, when they are loosed, who now injure so much while they are bound?

16. number. This number designates the crafty duplicity of the perverse army; and this may more easily be perceived in another translation, which says, "two myriads of myriads." This is the number which the parable of the Gospel opposes to the king who has ten thousand, as if the duplicity of the wicked resists the simple faith of Christ, for "thousands of thousands minister unto Him, and ten thousand times a hundred thousand stand before Him."

17. horses. The malignant spirits are involved in the same punishments with those over whose hearts they preside. For we read, that "they who worship the beast are to be tormented with fire and brimstone," and that "the smoke of their torments goes up for ages of ages." Observe, that in the plague of locusts, he said not that he saw horsemen, but only horses. For here the magnitude of the persecutions make manifest the presence of a contrary power. Lastly, here

there are heads of lions, but there there is the face of men, and the teeth alone of brutes. For heretics often make a shew of humanity, but the ministers of the last persecution exact by punishments even that which they recommend by words and signs.

mouths. He shews that he said "jacinth" for smoke. These things do not proceed visibly from their mouth; but they are the source of punishment to themselves and their hearers by their injurious preaching. "I will bring fire," he says, "out of the midst of thee, which is to devour thee."

19. tails. That is, in their speech and office. For "the prophet that teacheth a lie, he is the tail," for he conceals a part which is in a manner hidden and unclean by the volubility of a flattering tongue, saying to the ungodly, "Thou art good."

serpents. For the false teachers of the old serpent who deceived man, like those who are supported by the protection of princes, hurt more than if they persuaded by words alone. "He sitteth," he says, "lying in wait with the rich."

20. the rest. As he had described the false Christians and heretics, in order that he may comprehend the whole body of the devil, he now mentions also the error of the heathen, to whom it is of no avail not to have been slain by these plagues, as it is evident that they still continue in heathen wickedness. For not even in that last persecution will the heathen be compelled to yield their assent by the things mentioned above, but will die in their unbelief.

repented not. To an ungodly religion they add also an unholy manner of life. After he has described the cruelty of Antichrist, in order to shew his fall, he recapitulates in the usual way the commencement from the birth of Christ, and the glory of the Church.

ON CHAPTER 10

v. 1. angel. The Lord, the angel of the great counsel, comes down from heaven clothed with a cloud of flesh; as also Isaiah says, "Behold, the Lord rideth upon a swift cloud, and shall come into Egypt."

rainbow. That is, the promise of propitiation abiding around the good.

face. When the face of the Lord becomes bright, that is, when the knowledge of Him is manifested by the glory of the resurrection, His feet which are to preach glad tidings upon the mountains, and proclaim peace, are illumined with the fire of the Holy Spirit and are made firm like a pillar, for "James, Cephas, and John, seemed to be pillars," of the Church.

2. book. This is the book which was mentioned above, and which was closed by a long-continued covering, and was at last unfastened by the grace of the Lord, that, as the Prophet says, even "the deaf might hear the words of the book." And with reason is His face as the sun, because He now carries an open book.

earth. The preaching of the Christian faith is extended by land and sea. But, allegorically, the stronger members are placed in the greater dangers, the others in such as are suited to them. For God "does not suffer us to be tempted above that we are able."

3. thunders. When the Lord proclaims mightily, the Church also, filled with sevenfold grace, lifts up her voice to preach. For "the lion shall roar, who will riot fear? The Lord God hath spoken, who will not prophesy?" seeing that the seven thunders of which he is speaking are the same as the seven trumpets.

4. Seal. Neither do thou exhibit to all indiscriminately the mysteries of the Christian faith, lest they become of low esteem; nor close them to the good, lest they be entirely hidden. And for the same reason he heard at a later time, "Seal not the words of this prophecy." Both these are comprised in a single verse in Daniel, for it is said to him by the angel, "seal the book, and shut up the words even unto the time appointed."

5. hand. The angel swears by Him. who liveth for ever, while Christ, Who comes in the Father's Name, confirms the words of His own unchangeable truth, saying, "Heaven and earth shall pass away, but My words shall not pass away."

6. created. He who stands on the sea and on the earth, and stretches forth his hand to heaven, swears fitly by the Creator of the heaven, the earth, and the sea.

no longer. Assuredly, as the Psalmist says, "The time of the godly will bc for ever." But the changeable variety of secular times will cease at the last trumpet, for "the trumpet shall sound, and the dead shall arise incorrupt," and "their inheritance shall be for ever."

7. mystery. The mystery of the Gospel which is now preached will then be finished, when "the ungodly shall go into eternal punishment, but the righteous into eternal life."

8. voice. When the Lord lays open the mysteries of future time, and says, "For the kingdom of heaven is at hand," the Church also is admonished to receive the same book of preaching. But these words may also be suitable to John himself, who is to return to preaching after his banishment.

9. Give. Let him come to the Lord who wishes to receive the sacraments of teaching.

Take. That is, place it in thy inward parts, and write it down in the breadth of thy heart.

bitter. When thou hast received it, thou wilt be delighted by the sweetness of the divine oracle; but thou wilt perceive a bitterness on beginning to preach, and to practise what thou hast learned, or, at least, it is to be so understood according to Ezekiel, who, when he said that he had eaten the book, added, "And I went away in bitterness, in the indignation of my spirit."

11. prophesy. He shews what was signified by the book eaten up, and the sweetness mingled with bitterness, namely, that he was to be delivered from banishment, and was to preach the Gospel to the nations, which is sweet indeed through love, but is bitter through the persecutions that are to be endured.

ON CHAPTER 11

v. 1. reed. He received the office of writing the Gospel in the reed, which is not useless with a vain lustre, but is like "the rod of equity, the rod of the kingdom of God," for it describes the eternal kingdom of Christ.

Rise. "Rise," he said: not that John was seated, but that the hearts of all are aroused by this word to measure the writings and actions of the Gospel, for then they find what progress they each one make, and how far they agree with the divine rule.

worship. For not all they who are seen therein worship, as he "who shall confess Me." He commands, that is, in what he says, that a part should not be reckoned.

2. without. They who in name alone are united to the Church, and who neither draw near to the altar nor the most holy place, are cast forth by the rule of the Gospel, and are joined to the nations. For "all the glory of her who is the daughter of kings is from within."

tread. Not only are they driven from the Church, but they also fight against the Church itself, with the heathen as their allies, for three years and a-half. It is not that they only trample upon it then in the time of Antichrist; but that in that time all the body of the wicked, "in whom the ministry of iniquity already works," is joined as it were, to its own head.

3. witnesses. That the cruelty of the bad may not alarm the hearer, he mentions, that the Church also, which of two races is made one, is to become illustrious by the gift of miracles. The Church, too, ever contemplating its head, namely Christ, teaching in the flesh, will prophesy, it is said, for two years and a-half. For the months of three years and a-half, namely, thirty times forty-two, make up two hundred and sixty days. But Daniel writes, that the days of the same period in which the abomination of desolation is to be set up are one thousand two hundred and ninety.

sackcloth. That is, who are made to stand in penance; as the prophet says, "But I clothed myself in sackcloth of hair, while they were vexatious unto me."

4. olive trees. The Church is irradiated by the light of the two Testaments, and ever waits upon the commands of the Lord. So also the prophet Zechariah saw one candlestick with seven branches, and these two olive-trees, that is, testaments, pouring oil into the candlestick. This is the Church with its oil, which never fails, which makes it shine for the light of the world.

5. fire. If any one harms the Church, he is condemned by a retributive sentence of the same harm; and is consumed by fire. For "all they who take the sword shall perish with the sword." And so the Chaldean flame which was prepared for the children of God, slew the ministers of ungodliness themselves. Or: he who is to be changed for the better, is spiritually consumed in a good fire, by the prayers of the mouth of the Church. "Thou wilt heap," he says, "coals of fire upon his head."

6. power. All power in heaven and earth is given to the Church in Christ, for the keys of binding and loosing are committed to it. But spiritually also, the heaven is shut, that it rain no rain, in order that blessing from the Church may not come down upon the barren earth. As the Lord saith of the Father to His vineyard, "I will command the clouds that they rain no rain upon it."

waters. Not only do they make to cease the waters, but they also render those which had come down useless; and this is, to turn the waters into blood. The sweet savour of Christ, which comes with fragrance from the Church, is "to some a savour of death unto death, to others a savour of life unto life."

7. testimony. He shews clearly, that all these things take place before the last persecution, by saying, "when they shall have finished their testimony;" namely, that which they give, until the revelation of the beast, who is to come forth from the hearts of the ungodly. It is not that they do not then strive boldly to resist the enemy by the same testimony, but that the Church, as is supposed, will then be left destitute of the gift of miracles, while the adversary is resplendent with them in the sight of all through lying wonders. For, as the Lord says, "Want shall go before his face."

kill. He will overcome in those who shall succumb, he will kill in those who, with laudable patience, shall be slain. Or: if he shall overcome and kill spiritually, we may take it of a part of the witnesses, as the Lord says in the Gospel, "They will deliver you up to affliction, and kill you;" which Luke the Evangelist intimates to have been spoken of a part, saying, "Some of you they will kill."

8. bodies. "If they have persecuted Me," He says, "they will also persecute you." It is no wonder, then, if the city of the ungodly, which feared not to crucify the Lord, has His servants also in derision, even when they are slain. And such things as these ecclesiastical history relates to have often occurred.

Sodom. That is, "silent and dark," having forsooth neither the light of faith, nor the voice of confession. For "with the heart man believeth unto righteousness, and with the mouth confession is made unto salvation." These regions, for a sign of spiritual punishment, were visibly smitten with these plagues, that is, with devouring fire, and water turned into blood.

9. see. He said not the peoples and tribes will see, but, many from among the peoples who openly deride the saints, when others believe.

tombs. He has spoken of their wish and their opposition: not that they are able to effect that the Church should not be their memorial; as it is said, "Ye neither enter in, nor suffer others to enter in," seeing that some do enter in, although they oppose. But they will evidently effect, in respect of the bodies of the living and of the slain, that neither are the living suffered to meet together for their memory by the celebration of holy offices, nor the slain to have their names recited for their memory, nor to have their bodies buried for their memory as witnesses of God.

10. rejoice. As often as the righteous are afflicted, the unrighteous exult and feast, as, "while the ungodly is lifted up, the poor is consumed."

tormented. Because of the plagues with which the human race is vexed, because of their testimony to God, even the very sight of the righteous oppresses the unrighteous; as they themselves say, "He is grievous unto us even to behold."

11. days. Thus far the angel has spoken of the future, and now he brings in, as accomplished, that which he hears is to come to pass, namely that, after the reign of Antichrist has been destroyed, the saints have risen to glory.

fear. He has spoken of all the living, because even the righteous who shall remain alive will greatly fear at the resurrection of those who sleep.

12. cloud. This is the same that the Apostle said, "We shall be caught up in the clouds into the air, to meet the Lord."

enemies. Here he has distinguished the unrighteous from those of whom he had said, that they feared in common with them.

13. earthquake. When the terror of the judgment comes upon them, all the city of the devil, which is built upon the sand, with all its builders, will fall to the ground. For, both ten and seven are perfect numbers. But if it were not so, the whole would be to be understood from a part.

affrighted. Who of all men will boast that he has a pure heart, when "the powers of heaven shall be shaken."

gave glory. They are built upon a rock, who, from their own stability, glorify the Lord when others fall at the earthquake. For "the righteous will rejoice when he seeth the punishment of the wicked." Some understand the two prophets to be Enoch and Elijah, and that they are to preach for three years and a-half, and confirm the hearts of the faithful against the perfidy of Antichrist, which is presently to follow; and that, after their death, his cruelty is to rage for the same period of time, and then, when the conflict is at length renewed by the saints, who in the protection of their hiding-places were supposed to be dead, is to be overcome. And these, because of their fellowship in one body, are said to rise as prophets themselves; and when the persecution is intensified at the sight of those who were already thought to be dead, many of those who were supposed to be worthy of the number seven, or ten, will fall. For Daniel says, "He will confirm the covenant with many for one week, and in the half of the week the oblation and sacrifice will cease, and the abomination of desolation shall be in the temple;" and the following, "and when the abomination which makes desolate shall be set up, there will be a thousand two hundred and ninety days," which number is close upon the course of three years and a-half. Finally, Elijah of old destroyed his adversaries by fire, and was hidden for three years and a-half, and withheld the rain; and at length, when the false prophets were put to death, by means of the sacrifice which had been consumed, he turned Israel unto the Lord.

14. second. The second woe does not belong to the recapitulation, but to the battle of the horses, which was stirred up by the trumpet of the sixth angel; for the eagle had foretold three woes, from the voice of the three trumpets which was to come. But he did not utter it then, lest that which belongs to the seventh angel, and the end, should be supposed to follow immediately upon the third.

15. seventh. The six former trumpets, corresponding with the periods of the present age, announced the various conflicts of the wars of the Church. But the seventh, heralds in the eternal sabbath, and shews alone the victory and the dominion of the true King.

16. worshipped. Behold, he says, the third woe will come at the voice of the seventh angel. And when he had sounded, he only spoke of the Church as praising God and giving thanks, from which we understand that the retribution of the faithful will be nothing else than the woe of the evil ones.

17. who art. "Thou hast reigned from the age, although the ungodly are rebellious against Thee. But now that Thou art Judge, their fury will be repressed, and will cease." For, "The Lord hath reigned, let the people be angry."

18. dead. It agrees with the order, as we read in the Gospel, that first, indeed, all nations should be gathered together before the Judge, then that those on the right hand should be disposed in many mansions in the Kingdom of the

Father, but that the ungodly should be driven out beyond the limits of the kingdom, to be burned in the accursed flames.

corrupted. This is the last woe. Therefore, concerning the seven angels sounding with the trumpet, he now recapitulates from the birth of the Lord, as about to say the same things in another manner, and more comprehensively.

19. The temple of God, which was placed aforetime on the earth, had the ark of the covenant, inclosed within the mystical veil. But now, in the Church, which is "the temple of the living God," whose "conversation is in heaven," the ark of His Incarnation is laid open to the whole world, as the veil of the old temple, and the middle wall of partition, have been rent asunder by the blood of the Lord. For like the heavenly manna in clean gold is the Divinity in a holy body.

lightnings. These all are the miracles of the splendour, and preaching, and wars of the Church. He had said also that these things took place in the description of the announcement of the seven angels, from the Advent of the Lord, when He stood upon the altar, but generally from the begining to the end. Then he described particularly in what manner they took place, as he also does now, that the temple of God is opened in heaven, and that conflicts follow.

ON CHAPTER 12

v. 1. sign. It is the same sign which now also appears in the Church, that God is born of man.

a woman. The Church is clothed with the light of Christ, and treads upon temporal glory. "Righteousness," he says, "will arise in his days, and abundance of peace, until the moon be taken away, or consumed." That is, the abundance of peace will greatly increase, until it consume all the changeableness of mortality, and then death, the last enemy, will be destroyed. Or: because the same Church has partly the fruition of Christ, the Sun, in heaven, and is partly absent from the Lord, that which he says, "His left hand is under my head, and his right embraceth me," may be understood here.

stars. The Head of the Church is adorned with the number of the Apostles, which is twelve, whether Christ is understood, or whether the first beginning of the Church itself is designated under the name of the head. "Thou hast set," he says, "upon his head a crown of precious stone."

2. birth. The Church, in a spiritual sense, both brings forth those with whom it travails, and ceases not to travail with them when already born. As she herself says, "My little children, of whom I travail in birth again, until Christ be formed in you."

delivered. So the Lord says in the Gospel, "A woman, when she is in travail, hath sorrow because her hour is come, but when she hath brought forth a son, she remembers the anguish no more for joy." And He Himself expounded this to His disciples, and added, "And ye now, therefore, have sorrow, but I will see you again, and your heart shall rejoice."

3. dragon. The devil, blood-stained in his cruelty, is armed against the Church with the power of an earthly king. For in the seven heads he describes all his kings, and in the ten horns every kingdom.

4. tail. He intimates the power and malice of the enemy, whom the Church overcomes by the help of the Lord, for he has cast down an innumerable host of angels and men by deceptive testimony, as with a tail. For the tail is a part of

the body which is removed from sight, and unclean; and which conceals the parts which are unclean by the covering which it affords, that they may not appear. Tichonius, as his manner is, interprets the third part of the stars which fell, of false brethren, so that another third would be the Church, and the enemies external to it a third.

devour. The devil plots against the Church, and strives to extinguish the faith of Christ in the hearts of the faithful, that he may, as it were, kill him who has been taught, and to whom by teaching he has given birth. And a figure of this deceit was shewn in Herod, who, like an intestine foe, pretends that he desires to worship the Lord, in order that he may put Him to death.

5. man child. Although the dragon oppose, the Church ever brings forth Christ. But he spoke of the man child as conqueror of the devil, who had conquered the woman. For who but the man child, who is "to rule all nations with a rod of iron," rules the good with inflexible justice, breaks in pieces the bad? And this is also promised to the Church, in that it is said above, "I will give Him power over the nations, and He shall rule them with a rod of iron." For the Church, too, daily generates the Church, which rules the world in Christ.

caught up. Therefore ungodliness cannot apprehend Christ, Who is spiritually born in the minds of the hearers, because at the same time He reigns with the Father in heaven, "Who has raised up us also together with Him, and made us sit together in heavenly places in Christ."

6. wilderness. The Church rejoices in her sojourning in this present wilderness, as living in hope of things eternal. For she has received power to tread upon serpents and scorpions, and upon all the power of the red dragon, like the Israelitish multitude which was fed with heavenly bread, and overcame the fiery serpents by the sight of the serpent of brass.

place. "Be thou to me," he says, "as God my protector, and as a place of refuge, that I may be safe."

days. In this number of days, which makes three years and a-half, he comprehends all the times of Christianity, because Christ, Whose body the Church is, preached the same length of time in the flesh.

7. heaven. The heaven signifies the Church, in which he says that Michael, with his angels, fights against the devil, for that, according to the will of God, he contends for the Church in her sojourning, by praying and ministering help; of whom Daniel also said, that he would come to the aid of the Church in the last and most grievous affliction; from which they suppose that Antichrist is to be slain by him. And they are said to be his angels in the same way

that our angels also are. For the Lord says, "Their angels do always behold the face of My Father," the angels, that is, of those whose citizens they are.

fought. The angels of Satan are not those alone who are like him in nature and will, but men who are entangled in their snares are also to be understood.

8. prevailed not. That is, they prevailed not through all time.

found. It was not found, that is, in holy men, who, by his expulsion from them, have already become a heaven themselves, and who through faith no more receive him back, who has once been expelled.

9. earth. The old enemy, who is expelled from the spiritual, is more closely shut up in the earthly. This is to be hurled down from heaven, and sent into the earth. For to him it is said, "Earth shalt thou eat all the days;" and in this earth he is bruised by the feet of the saints, as it is written, "Thou shalt tread upon the asp and the basilisk."

10. salvation. It is clearly shewn in what heaven these things take place, for we know that in the Church salvation is procured by the victory of Christ, and because of this He says, "All power is given to Me in heaven and in earth;" not that power which He Himself always had, but that which He began to have in the Church, as the Head in the members, from the time that He Himself willed.

brethren. The angels express joy at the salvation of their brethren, that is, of those who will become citizens, but who now are strangers.

accused. For he suggests, that they both make an ill-use of prosperity, and have not patience in adversity.

11. lives. With good reason do they despise their lives for Christ's sake, who have overcome so great an adversary by the blood of Christ.

12. rejoice. Here, by dwellers in heaven, must be understood both angels and holy men, and it belongs to both to rejoice in the Lord, since both men are joined with angels, and angels minister to man's nature in Christ.

Woe. As he has shewn that joy is to be the expectation of the redeemed, so, also, is lamentation of those who perish. And a great woe is impending over those of whom the most wicked enemy has possession in his wrath.

13. saw. The devil assails the Church with inextricable craft, and the more he is cast down, so much the more does he persecute.

14. wings. The Church is upheld by the two Testaments, and avoids the envenomed tumult of the world, and seeks in the affection of her mind the solitude of a "meek and quiet spirit," while she thus sings with joy, "Behold I got me away far off in flight, and abode in the wilderness." Nor does it make any difference that there she asks for the wings of a dove, but here receives those of an eagle. For as the Church, "whose youth is renewed as an eagle's," is

represented in the former because of the gift of the Holy Spirit, so also is it in the latter, because of the lofty flight and heavenly vision, by which it beholds God with a clean heart.

nourished. The whole time of the Church is signified, as being comprised in the number of the days above. For a "time" denotes one year, "times" two, "half a time" six months.

15. flood. Water signifies the vehemence of persecutors; whence it is said, "Perhaps like water they would have swallowed us up." So, then, the Church is not only raised up by the word of God, but is driven onward by the violence of persecution, and hastens to fly away from the earth.

16. swallowed. The holy earth is the flesh of the Lord, which by swallowing up death which it accepted, and which for a time prevailed against it, has taught us also to swallow up death. The Church may also be understood, by the warnings and prayers of whose mouth the plots of the enemy are avoided.

17. wroth. When he saw that the persecutions could not be continued, because they were averted by the mouth of the holy earth, he prepared himself the more to rest upon the mystery of iniquity, that he might be able to plot continually.

commandments. To keep the commandments of God in the faith of Jesus Christ is to fight with the dragon, and provoke him to battle; and thanks be to God, Who has made the attempts of the cruel dragon of no effect. For, behold, while he endeavoured to annihilate the Lord incarnate, he is defeated by His resurrection. Afterwards, by striving to deprive the Apostles of their boldness in teaching, he was urgent, as it were, to take away from the world the woman, that is, the whole Church. But as he has laboured in vain to effect this, he assails indiscriminately every age of the faithful. And so it is, as follows.

18. sea. That is, the same enemy, when he is to excite plotting and war, stands upon the multitude of the people, "which the wind scattereth away from the face of the earth," and which is wont to accept his devices.

ON CHAPTER 13

v. 1. beast. The beast has different interpretations, according to its place. Here, accordingly, it denotes the body of the devil, which springs from the people of the ungodly; for this is the sea, which above is understood as the abyss. And, therefore, the dragon is said to be king of all that is in the waters, and whose "heads," according to David, "are broken in pieces in the sea.

horns. He shews that the seven heads are the same as the ten horns. For he had said, that the dragon bore seven diadems upon ten heads. But now he says that the beast has ten diadems upon ten horns. For seven and ten are the same, as "he will receive sevenfold in this world," when another evangelist has a "hundredfold."

blasphemy. For they call their kings gods, as well those who are dead, and as it were translated to heaven, and among the gods, as those also who have the name of Augustus upon earth, which with them expresses deity. But in another place he says, that the whole beast itself is full of blasphemy.

2. leopard. He is represented as like a leopard, because of the diversity of the nations; a bear, because of his malice and fury; a Hon, because of his strength of body and pride of tongue. We read in Daniel of the kingdom of the Chaldæans being compared to a lioness, of the Persians to a bear, of the Macedonians to a leopard.

power. So the Apostle, speaking of the body of the devil, says, "Whose coming is after the working of Satan, in all power, and signs, and prodigies of falsehood, in those who perish."

3. heads. Antichrist, who pertains to the heads of the earthly kingdom, by imitation of our true Head, dares to exhibit himself as one who has been slain, and has risen again, and who is to be accepted as Christ, Who truly accomplished this. And the falsehood of this pretence is said to have been anticipated in the instance of Simon Magus.

wondered. He puts the genus for the species, in saying that the beast was worshipped, seeing that earthly men were to worship the counterfeit head itself under the name of the Head, Who was truly slain, and alive.

4. worshipped. They say that they worship God, Who gave power to Christ.

like. They themselves say, Who is like Christ? Or who can overcome Him?

5. mouth. "Who is exalted," he says, "above all that is called God."

blasphemies towards. For he does not blaspheme with open mouth, until three years and a-half, but in the mystery of iniquity, which, when a difference is made, and the man of sin is revealed, will be disclosed. And then he will say, "I am Christ;" whereas now it is, "Lo, here is Christ," or, "Lo there." Again, "towards God" signifies "against God."

6. tabernacle. The wicked one usurps the dignity of the name of God, and he will presume to call the Church also his own.

7. saints. By the whole, he denotes a part which can be overcome, when in the violence of the time, even the elect, if it be possible, will be shaken; that the Jews may be condemned, who did not believe the truth, but accepted a lie.

8. dwell. He said "all," but "who dwell on the earth." For, "They who depart from Thee," he says, "shall be written in the earth."

book. It is just, that they who serve the author of death should not be written in the book of life, and that they who are deluded by the fictitious death of the beast, should be without the fellowship of "the Lamb, Who has taken away the sins of the world." "Of the Lamb," he says, as in what follows.

beginning. "A lamb," that is, as Peter says, "without spot, who verily was fore-ordained before the foundation of the world, but was manifested in these last times. Another version has translated it, "the lamb sealed from the beginning of the world." It may also be understood by transposition, that the names of the saints were written from the beginning in the book of life.

9. have an ear. As often as the Scripture interposes this saying, it seeks an attentive hearer, because of the obscurity of the subject. For in order that the shortlived kingdom of the devil may not be highly esteemed, he anticipates the thoughts of man by saying, "He that shall lead into captivity will go into captivity;" that is, the devil with the beast who now appears to lead the nations captive in his toils, will himself speedily be in captivity with his own.

10. sword. He who now persecutes the Church with carnal or even spiritual death, him the Lord Jesus "will slay with the breath of His mouth, and will destroy with the brightness of His coming."

patience. He had promised that the slayer of men should be killed. But because "no one is crowned but he who has striven lawfully," he says now that there is need of courage, now of a firm breast. After the beast has been described generally, first in hypocrisy, then in the open mouth of blasphemies, he describes it also in the persons of the leaders alone, in like manner in hypocrisy, then as revealed.

11. another. He has called him another, from his office, otherwise he is the same. But that which is here the sea, is, as Daniel testifies, the earth; for as he saw four beasts come up out of the sea, it was said to him, "These four great beasts are four kingdoms, which shall arise out of the earth."

horns. He shews the horns of a lamb, that he may secretly introduce the poison of the dragon. For by the false assumption of sanctity, which the Lord truly had in Himself, he pretends that a matchless life and wisdom are his. Of this beast the Lord says, "Beware of false prophets, which come to you in sheep's clothing, but inwardly are ravening wolves."

12. power. The wretched disciples follow their master in everything.

causeth. He shews the power of seduction, in that he made subject to himself both the body and the soul which dwells in it.

healed. That is, who pretended that by rising again he had overcome death. For the Scripture had spoken of him not as "slain," but "as it were slain;" as was said of the Jews, "that they entered not into the Prætorium, lest they should be defiled." For the Evangelist did not affirm that the most polluted could have been polluted if they had entered the Prætorium, nor did the Jews who were guilty of so great crimes really fear to be polluted. But he related what they had simulated, as if affirming it.

13. fire. He preferred the miracle of fire, as if the greatest, to all others, that, as the Lord Christ had given to His disciples the gift of divers miracles by the Holy Ghost, Who came in fire, so he with deceitful craft might delude his own, as it were, by a similar gift.

14. seduces. "His coming win be," as is said, "after the working of Satan in all power, and signs, and prodigies of falsehood." And there is wont to be a question, whether these are called "signs and prodigies of falsehood," because he is to deceive the senses of men by phantasms, so as to seem to do what he does not; or because these very things, even if they shall be true prodigies, will lead to falsehood those who shall believe, that they could only have been wrought by divine influence, being ignorant of the power of the devil. For it was not by a phantastical, but a true fire and whirlwind that he destroyed so great a household as that of the holy Job, with so great flocks. But whether they are called "prodigies of falsehood" in this way or that, it is in this that the temptation will appear to be greater than all the rest, that when the pious

martyr submits his body to torments he too at the same time performs so many miracles before his eyes.

image. That is, that they should be like him, and make an image for him, "as he has the wound from the sword and lives," as another version expresses it. This is that they say so falsely, that they have been dead and have risen again with Antichrist, as to imply that he too makes God a mediator between himself and his own, whereas he has not like our Lord Jesus Christ another one, between whom and himself he may be a mediator.

15. breath. That is, by making himself an image of the beast, he pretended that he gave the spirit of truth to the very people in whom the falsehood was fulfilled.

speak. Not only will he delude the wretched multitude by counterfeiting the spirit with fire, but he will also make it of use for teaching others.

16. mark. The mark is the mystery of iniquity, which is received by those who are hypocrites in practice and profession.

17. buy. By this mention of buying and selling, he teaches, that as the Church has delivered the Creed for good, to be profitable to our salvation; so they for evil confine themselves within such a definition as this, that there be licence given neither of buying, nor of selling, even as merchants who sail in the same ship, are bound by an uniform signal.

name. That is, who participates in his deceit. For the mark, that is, the note and name of the beast and the number of his name are one. And it is the number of a man, that we may not suppose him, as the opinion of some is, to be either the devil, or a demon, but one from among men, in whom Satan is to dwell bodily. For he is "the man of sin, the son of perdition."

18. number. This number among the Greeks, is said to be found in the name of Titan, that is, "a giant" in this manner,—T three hundred, E five, I ten, T three hundred, A one, N fifty. And it is thought that Antichrist will usurp this name, as if he excelled all in power, boasting also that he is the one of whom it was written, "He rejoiced as a giant to run his course. His going forth is from the highest heaven." And Primasius also mentions another name, which contains the same number,—A one, N fifty, T three hundred, E five, M forty, O seventy, Σ two hundred, which signifies, "contrary to honour." Besides there is the word,—A one, P one hundred, N fifty, O seventy, Y four hundred, M forty, E five, that is, "I deny." By these, both the character of the person and the asperity of the work of Antichrist are indicated. But how so great a coveter of praise should be willing to be denoted by such a mark, requires a lengthened exposition. Otherwise: who is ignorant, that the number six, in accordance with which the world was created, signifies the perfection of

work? And this, whether simple, or multiplied by ten, or a hundred, demonstrates the fruit of the same perfection to be sixty-fold, or a hundred-fold. The weight of gold also which was brought to Solomon every year was six hundred and sixty-six thousand talents. The seducer, therefore, will presume to exact for himself the offering which is rightfully due and paid to the true king.

ON CHAPTER 14

v. 1. Lamb. That is, when this Church was toiling under the burden of its conflicts, the Lord Jesus Christ preserved it by the example of His power, and the defence of His protection. For when the body had been shewn which was confounded by the power of the dragon, and marked by his brand, he shews the Church rejoicing in its wonted splendour and numbers, that thou shouldest not be afraid lest the body of the Lamb had succumbed to the fury of the beast. And observe, that the beast stands on the sand of the sea, the Lamb on Mount Zion.

thousand. This finite number ought to be understood as infinite, and, by the signification of the hidden mystery, as suited to the virgin band, which loves God from the whole heart, the whole soul, and the whole mind; and to the body also, which consists of four qualities, and is in its integrity consecrated to Him. For three times three are nine, and four times four sixteen, and sixteen times nine make one hundred and forty-four. So, then, when from among those who are established in the merit of carnal life, and appear on Mount Zion with the Lamb, there is perceived so perfect a multitude, no doubt can exist concerning the other members of the Church.

foreheads. He shews what is the imitation of the mark on the forehead of the body of the beast, while he says that God and Christ were written on the foreheads of the Church.

2. waters. The loud voice of the saints is the great devotion of love, which he states that he heard from heaven, in saying that they who uttered the voice "stood on Mount Zion." For he intended to shew that by Mount Zion he meant no other than the Church, which, in order to overcome the grievances of its afflictions, is exalted by the sublime delight of contemplation, and celebrates at once by praise and by imitation the conflicts of her King. For this is in truth to sing unto the Lamb Who stands.

harpers. When all the saints are God's harpers, for "by crucifying the flesh with its vices and lusts" they praise Him on the psaltery and harp; how much more are they who, by the privilege of evangelical chastity, make themselves altogether a perfect sacrifice to the Lord, and who, in a special manner, "deny themselves," and "take up their cross," and follow the Lamb whithersoever He goeth?

3. song. The old song was, "Blessed is He Who hath His dwelling in Zion, and His household in Jerusalem." But the new song is, "Rejoice thou barren, that barest not;" and again He says, "I will give to my eunuchs in my house, and within my walls, a name better than of sons and daughters."

able. In a special manner to sing a song unto the Lamb is to rejoice with Him for ever, even above all the faithful, because of the incorruption of the flesh. And yet the rest of the elect are able to hear this song, although they cannot utter it, because, through love, they still rejoice for their exaltation, if they do not rise up to their rewards.

4. virgins. The blessed Augustine has set forth this very beautifully in his exhortation to virgins, saying, "Go on, ye holy youths and maidens of God, ye men and women, celibate and unmarried, go on perseveringly unto the end. Praise the Lord more sweetly, Whom ye think of more frequently. Hope in Him more auspiciously, Whom ye serve more constantly. Love Him more ardently, Whom ye please more attentively. With loins girded, and lights burning, wait for the Lord, when He comes from the marriage. Ye will bring to the marriage of the Lamb a new song, which ye will sing upon your harps, such an one indeed as no one but ye will be able to utter. For so one saw you in the Apocalypse, who, above all others, was beloved of the Lamb, who was wont to lie upon His breast. He himself saw you, as twelve thousand holy harpers, of undefiled virginity of the body, of inviolate truth in the heart. Ye follow the Lamb, for virginal also is the flesh of the Lamb. Ye follow Him in virginity of heart and flesh, whithersoever He may go. For what is to follow, but to imitate? Because "Christ suffered for us, leaving you an example, that ye should follow His steps." "

firstfruits. They are chosen by the Holy Spirit for the merits of their will, as holier and purer victims, from the holy and immaculate flock of the Church. For the Apostle, having no commandment of the Lord concerning them, implores them that they "present their bodies a living sacrifice, holy, acceptable to God."

5. guile. Virgins are not united to the divine company by the merit of chastity alone, if they have not also a life free from all contagion of sin. Tichonius does not interpret this vision of virgins specially, but of the whole Church generally, which the Apostle "betrothes to one husband, to present it a pure virgin to Christ;" and he concludes thus: "He said not, There was no lie in

their mouth, but, 'there was not found;' as the Apostle says, 'And this indeed ye were, but ye were washed, and, 'The iniquity of the unjust will not hurt him, in the day when he shall turn from his iniquity,' and he can be a virgin, and 'deceit not be found in his mouth.' For by virgins he means the chaste and modest."

6. flying. As he had described the doubtful and varied fight of the Church with the dragon, as she is a sojourner in the age, it remains to assign a due recompence to both the combatants, and shew what punishments await the bad, or what rewards the good. So, then, the preacher who runs hither and thither through the midst of the Church, carries with him the Gospel of the eternal kingdom.

preach. It is fitting that they who are lifted up by a heavenly flight, should also, through preaching, raise up their earthly minds from the seat of their torpidness.

nation. "This Gospel," He says, "shall be preached in all the world, and then shall the end come."

7. Fear. Do ye look forward the more to your own salvation, he says, the more speedy is the retribution which awaits you, which is unchangeable for ever. For ye fear the Lord, the Maker of the world, and not the momentary tyranny of the beast.

8. Babylon. He says that the ruinous city of the devil has already fallen; and this may be after the manner of Scripture, which is wont to represent as past that which it knows is inevitably to be fulfilled; or perhaps the proud were cast down by the Lord, when they were puffed up by the devil, as the Psalmist says, "Thou castedst them down, while they were lifted up."

nations. The ungodly city, which is gathered from all nations, itself makes the nations, that is, its own members, drunk with the wine of error. But the city of the Lord, which cultivates the vine of Sorek, does not desire to "be drunk with wine, wherein is excess," lest it be deprived of the promised denarius of life.

9. worship. That is, who shall have worshipped the beast, and the head, which was, as it were, slain

mark. By saying, "on his forehead, or on his hand," he shews that the devil marks some by an unholy profession, but others by practice alone.

10. drink. In that he says, "he also shall drink," he shews that there is another also who has drunk, so as not to exclude him who, although he is not visibly mingled with the nations, yet worships the beast under the name of Christ. But they are justly laid low by the cup of the Lord, who give to drink the cup of the wrath of fornication, not, according to Jeremiah, that they may

vomit forth the malice of a heart which is to be cleansed, but that they may be condemned, and perish by falling asleep in eternal death.

tormented. The saints who reign with the Lord are always able to see the punishment of the wicked, that they may for ever sing the mercies of the Lord, and so render to their deliverer the greater thanks. For the sight of the torments of the wicked does not grieve those who are of the same mind with the just Judge, as neither was the sight of the rest of Lazarus able to cool the rich man who was buried in flames.

11. night. They say that the lion spares a prostrate man. But this beast is fiercer than a lion, and the more he is worshipped, so much the greater punishment does he inflict.

receive. St. Augustine interprets the beast as the ungodly city, and the image of the beast as the likeness of a bird; of those, that is, who are Christians by a deceitful appearance; and the mark, as the note of guilt, which he says is worshipped, and is subject to him, and in agreement with him.

12. patience. Although the beast has vented his rage, yet the saints are not made sad by the temporal suffering which is to be rewarded by eternal bliss. For they see, on the other hand, that their persecutors, who for a time act proudly, suffer eternal punishments with the beast.

13. voice. Beautiful is now the agreement of those who speak. For behold, this one proclaims that the kingdom of the Lord is at hand, that one that the city of the devil is fallen, a third announces the flames of the ungodly, another the rest of the blessed; and he both utters his voice from heaven, and commands it as worthy of eternal memory, to be committed to writing. For "the righteous rejoice because their names are written in heaven," but the ungodly "are blotted out of the book of the living."

dead. I thank Thee, O Jesus, Who makest blessed in heaven those who die in Thee on earth, and how much more those who lay down their blissful lives both in and for Thy faith!

labours. As he had said that the ungodly have no rest for ever, so, on the contrary, he shews that the faithful, who are helped by their former works, from henceforth rest, that is, from the time of death. For, "when He has given His beloved sleep, this is the inheritance of the Lord." But "the sluggard would not plough because of the cold, therefore shall he beg in harvest, and there shall not be given to him."

14. cloud. Thus far has the voice of the harlot been premised, and it now remains to exhibit the person of the Judge Himself, Who, when He comes to judgment, overshadows the glory of His divinity by a cloud of flesh, that the ungodly "may see Him Whom they pierced."

crown. He has described above what this cloud is, in the appearance of the woman, and the crown of twelve stars upon her head. But it may also signify the victory of Him Who reigns.

sickle. This is the judicial sentence of separation, which cannot by any means whatever be avoided. For we are within it, whithersoever we attempt to flee, for whatsoever is enclosed by the sickle falls within it.

15. angel. The angels, of whom we read in the Gospel as "the reapers of the earth," are all sent forth to minister for those who have the inheritance of salvation," and they take account of the several merits of the Church, and report them daily to the Lord.

reap. Behold, He says, "Through iniquity abounding, the love of many has waxed cold," and through the burning heat of evils falling upon it, the harvest of the earth has now almost ceased to be green. So, then, for the elect's sake, the days are shortened, in order that grains already ripe may not fall off. And do thou commit the tares and the chaff to the flames, but the heavenly fruit to the garners of bliss.

17. another. If Christ appeared on the white cloud as the reaper, is the grape-gatherer but the same, finely repeated because of the twofold fruit of the Church? For "He Who sowed seed in His field" also Himself "planted a vineyard in a fruitful place." But the planting degenerated, because of the negligence of those who kept it.

18. fire. The office of the angels, as Jerome says, is twofold. For some assign rewards to the righteous, while others preside over the several torments; as it is said, "Who maketh His angels spirits, and His ministers a burning fire." The two angels who proclaim that the harvest is dry, and the corn ripe, may be understood to be the prayers of the Church, which, with a great voice, that is, with a great desire, prays daily that the kingdom of the Lord may come, and with these words.

Thrust in. As the harvest, so also the vintage is partly earthly, partly heavenly. But the maturity of both indicates the end of the world.

ripe. That is, her sins are complete. But the perfection of the good may also be called ripeness. For, as the holy Gregory says, although the end of the world depends on its own course, yet by overtaking such as are more perverse, because they are deservedly overwhelmed in its ruin, it becomes known through them.

19. sickle. He who has the sickle of the reaper has also that of the grape-gatherer. For the judgment is one, and will take place at one time; but in the harvest and the vintage he shews the beginning and the end of the same affliction.

winepress. If this harvest also of the vintage pertain only to the bad, the winepress signifies punishment; but if to the good as well, the treading of the winepress, as the threshing of the floor, crushes what is useless, and proves what is of use. And so the Apostle says that the precious metals are preserved by fire, while the hay and the stubble are consumed, both which are done without the heavenly Jerusalem. But the winepress of wrath is so named in the same form of speech, as it is said, "The Lord delivered him in the evil day."

20. blood. There went forth vengeance, even to the rulers of the people. For in the last contest there went forth vengeance even to the devil and his angels, because of the blood of the saints which was shed; as it is written, "In blood thou hast sinned, and blood pursueth thee." Concerning the horses, it has been spoken above.

hundred. That is, through all the four parts of the world. For quaternity is multiplied by itself, as in the four faces with four sides, and the wheels. Tichonius interprets the reaper and the grape-gatherer of the Church, as it becomes glorious after the flames of persecution, and holds the power of binding and loosing. The angel from the temple, or the altar, proclaims the empire of the blood-red Lord, not with open voice, but by the suggestion of the Holy Spirit, Whose operation is in His body, and shews that it is now the time for the bad to be accursed; and he has power over the fire, namely, that which went forth from the mouth of the witnesses, and devoured their adversaries. Thus far concerning the conflict of the Church, and the perfect end of either contest.

BOOK THE THIRD

ON CHAPTER 15

v. 1. sign. Again the order is renewed. And as in he were about to relate the same plagues of the last persecution, he wished the hearer to be made attentive, in that he said, "a sign great and marvellous."

seven. That is to say, the Church which is replete with sevenfold grace.

last. He calls them "the last," because in them the wrath of God is consummated. For the wrath of God ever smites the rebellious people with seven plagues. He says repeatedly in Leviticus, "And I will smite you with seven plagues." And these are to be the last, when the Church shall have come forth from the midst of it.

2. glass. That is, the pellucid fount of Baptism, which is consecrated by the fire of the Holy Ghost. Or else: because it pertains to the nature of fire, in that it is made red by martyrdom.

victory. They who overcome the wiles of the beast, appear in consequence to stand upon a baptism of fire. For they desire, as the Apostle says, "to contend earnestly for the faith once delivered unto the saints."

harps. That is, they have the hearts of those who praise dedicated to God, and melodious with the truth of both Testaments; or, the flesh extended on the wood of passion. And here, not the sound of the voice alone is signified, but the operation of a good work.

3. Great and marvellous. I have found this song in both Testaments, where the Lord, both true and merciful, is celebrated as the Judge Who is to be worshipped by all ages.

5. temple. He repeats what he had set forth before, and the vision accords with the song. For, in order that the Lord may be worshipped by all nations, the temple of the mysteries of God, formerly inclosed within the walls of one city, now begins to be opened spiritually to the world.

6. came. This is the same with that which Mark says, "But they went forth, and preached everywhere."

linen. "As many of you," the Apostle says, "as have been baptized into Christ have put on Christ." For "He is the chief corner-stone, elect." Or, if the singular be understood to be put for the plural, it signifies various ornaments of virtues. Another translation has, "white linen," which indicates mortification of the flesh in teachers, according to this, "I chastise my body, and subject it to servitude, lest perchance, while preaching to others, I myself be found reprobate."

girdle. Let him who desires to preach strong things not only mortify the body, but also bind the breast with the gold of wisdom. Or, at least, to bind the breasts with golden girdles, is to restrain all the motions of changeful thoughts by the bands of the love of God alone.

7. seven vials. These are the bowls which are carried with their odours by the living creatures and the elders, who are the Church, and who are also the seven angels. The same bowls are said to contain both the sweetness of supplications, and the wrath of punishments. For they are poured forth by the saints before the advent of the kingdom of God, when the judgments of God, which are now no longer secret as the abyss, but open as the bowls, are announced as being salvation to the righteous, but destruction to the ungodly. As the Apostle says, "Because we are unto God a sweet savour of Christ in those who are saved, and in those who perish."

8. smoke. The Church, when it is to preach to the nations, is first influenced itself with the fire of love, and sends forth the smoke of pious confession, while it "gives thanks to God for His unspeakable gift."

enter. No one is able to be incorporated among the members of the Church, but he who hears the mysteries of faith from the preachers, and learns that Jesus is constituted by God the Judge both of the living and the dead. But if thou shalt interpret the smoke to be the secret judgment of God, these remain impenetrable, and closed to mortal men "until," after the plagues of the present age are ended, "the Lord come, Who is both to bring to light even the hidden things of darkness, and make manifest" how much the coming of Antichrist confers which is either of utility in proving the faith of the Church, or of judgment in blinding the eyes of the Jews, "Who received not the love of the truth, that they might be saved."

ON CHAPTER 16

v. 1. pour out. Power was given to the Church to impose judgment upon those who are to be condemned, and to give absolution in mercy to those who are converted. And to all the angels indeed was the command given, to pour upon the earth. But the same men of earth, according to the difference of sins, have different appellations assigned, that the fulness of guilt also might be reckoned by the number seven, as well as that of preaching and vengeance.

2. earth. Preachers pour out the wrath of God in a twofold manner, while they either impose the punishments of the ungodly upon the ungodly themselves by judging spiritually; as Peter said to Simon, "Thy money perish with thee;" or they manifest it to holy Church by preaching, as he also said, "For their judgment now of a long time lingereth not, and their perdition slumbereth not." A third manner may also be understood, in that each sinner, as the preaching of the truth is heard, is destroyed by the severer wound of contradiction, of which the Lord said, "If I had not come and spoken unto them, they had not had sin."

Lore. They who forsake the lord, and worship the devil, will spiritually perish from the most grievous wound of the same ungodliness.

3. sea. They who not only are stamped with the mark of Antichrist, but who also assail the stedfastness of the servants of Christ with the waves of bitter persecution, will be punished with a spiritual retribution which he calls blood; and they who boasted that they were alive, will be proved to have served the author of death.

4. waters. And they also who pretend that they give to drink sweet things, in order that they may pour out their poison upon the incautious, will be punished with the worthy retribution of a continual plague.

angel. In the angel of the waters he speaks of all the angels of the peoples, who in inner affection are united in singing the praises of God; for that inavenging the blood of His servants, He has made their murderers to drink of death.

7. judgments. That which the angels are, the same also is the altar giving thanks to God, that is, the inner affection of saints, or angels, or men, who bear rule over the peoples by teaching.

8. sun. The persecutors of the Church, who, like the fiery sun, strive to dry up the seed of the word of God, are to be burned in the future with the fire of hell. Or, if thou interpret the sun of the brightness of the wise, it is not given to the angel who pours out upon the waters to scorch men with heat and with fire, but to the same sun. For while the wise, overcome by torments, are infected by the error of evil doing, the weak, induced by their example, are inflamed with temporal desires. But the heat, as we said, may also be understood to be, that the body of the devil is incurably tormented and incited to blasphemy by the stedfastness of the saints, of which the prophet says, "Wrath takes hold of the people without understanding," and "now fire devours the adversaries." And that "now" forsooth, for indeed the fire of the last judgment is reserved.

9. men. At the present time indeed, so far as is permitted, the devil glorifies his own, which glory and joy the Holy Spirit has described to be plagues and sorrows. For we read also above, that the army of the devil killed men with fire, smoke, and brimstone; not that he killed them openly, but that he doomed those who are consentient with him to these flames.

10. seat of the beast. The seat of the beast, that is, his kingdom, as it were the judiciary power, is darkened by plagues of this kind, that is, by the false joy of earthly felicity, and is made to be without light; as the Psalm has, "Thou didst cast them down, while they were lifted up." For he said not, after they were lifted up.

tongues. As the righteous "will eat the labours of his own hands," so the ungodly also, exposed to the just punishments of his blasphemy, is satiated as it were with his own tongue. They hurt themselves therefore who blasphemed, because of the wrath of God, with which when they were pierced through, they thought it joy.

11. repented not. He referred it not to their own hardness, but to the just indignation of God, Who sent on them a plague of such a kind, that in it they should not remember themselves. For who, when afflicted in body, does not feel the hand of God, like Antiochus. "They blasphemed," he said, that is, not openly, but by luxuriating in sins.

12. Euphrates. While the people perish, the affluence of Babylon, in which there is nothing living, nothing green, which is not fit for fire, will remain. This is the same that he said above, "The harvest of the earth is dried," the saints of the king hasten to meet the Sun of Righteousness. Otherwise: as "while the ungodly is lifted up, the poor is consumed," so when the pestilent is

scourged, the wise will become more astute. And now, in his accustomed manner, he passes over the seventh angel, and recapitulates briefly from the beginning

13. frogs. The spirit of the devil, and of Antichrist, and of those who are set over his body, which is spoken of as threefold, according to the number of the parts of a body, is compared with frogs, to creatures, that is, which are horrible in their haunts, their appearance, and their vexatious croaking, which although they seem to be inhabitants of the waters, yet move about in filth and mud. For hypocrites indeed, while they promise their own the water of life, lie dead and hidden beneath the filth which believers deposit in the water. So Pharaoh, who to destroy the people at their Baptism went in after them, was therein slain.

14. demons. For as was done by the magicians of Pharaoh, so is it to be supposed that these will perform signs. And not without reason did he remember these, when he had made mention of frogs, but that he might announce that the ministers of Satan would then also perform similar signs. For the magicians were permitted to prevail by their enchantments as far as the sign of frogs.

kings. As there are holy kings to whom, when the Euphrates is dried, the way of the East is laid open; so also are there said to be evil kings of the earth, who, without being gathered together from the whole world into one place, but each nation in its place, are to fight against the saints. By "the great day of the Lord," he means the whole time from the Lord's Passion. "The day" may also be taken to be the day of judgment, when the army of the devil, which has been gathered together through the whole time of the present life, will meet the Lord, the King, that it may be overthrown.

15. I come. Another version has more suitably, "At the great day of God Almighty: behold He cometh as a thief."

Blessed. Blessed are they whose sins are covered, who hide the baseness of a reprehensible life before the eyes of the just at the judgment, by the covering of subsequent good works. In the Gospel also, the Lord, under the example of the thief to be guarded against, commands His servants to watch.

16. Hermagedon. Elsewhere he explains this place, saying, "He gathered them together to battle, and they compassed the camp of the saints and the chosen city," that is, the Church. On the contrary, the seat of the ungodly one, the devil, may also be understood, who in the man of perdition, inflated with the pride of usurped Deity, will rejoice to resume his former plotting, which was formerly interdicted by the Lord. For Hermagedon is interpreted, the "rising up together to former things," or, "the round mountain."

17. air. Above, the blood of vengeance went forth as far as the bridles of the horses, namely, the unclean spirits; and so here, when the same final vengeance was poured upon the same aërial powers, it is said that "it is done," that is, that the end is come, when, as the Apostle says, "the last enemy, death, shall be destroyed." Thus far, under the name of "plagues," the last persecution is described; all which Tichonius will have to be understood in a contrary way. "It is, 'the plague which cannot be healed,' he says, and 'the great wrath,' to receive the power of sinning in an especial manner against the saints, and not as yet to be overtaken by the greater wrath of God. The accession of blessedness indeed, is the death of the wicked, as on the contrary, torments and humiliation are the glory of the Church. For at that very time all the ungodly will be unhurt by any plague of the body, as they who have received all power to rage. Nor in the completion of sins, and the consummation of wrath, will there then be need that any one of the wicked should be scourged and restrained from fury. He recapitulates from the same persecution, and describes the fall of the ungodly city."

18. lightnings. At the end of the world, when there shall be such tribulation as has not been from the beginning, the greatest signs will in like manner be shewn, but whether on the side of the good, or on the side of the bad, or on both sides, as it was in the instance of Moses and the magicians of Pharaoh, is not here sufficiently apparent.

19. divided. The ungodly city wages a threefold war against the Church of Christ. For the heathen and Jews attack it in open conflict, heretics by treacherous defection, false brethren by evil examples. And this has been represented above in the three bad horses, red, black, and pale.

cities. That is to say, all the strength and confidence of the nations. For the mirth of the ungodly is their great fall, and the joy of the unjust their destruction.

wrath. Babylon then falls, or drinks the wrath of God, when it receives power against Jerusalem, especially at the last. Therefore he says that it has fallen by the earthquake, which He makes for the Church. But if thou shalt refer it to the day of judgment, the ungodly, who now says in his heart, "God hath forgotten," will then come into remembrance with God.

20. island. The Church, which from the height of its stability is compared with islands and mountains, prudently hides itself from the waves of the persecutors.

21. hail. The hail of the wrath of God is likened to a talent; for it is both heavy in weight, and equal in judgment, and is inflicted upon all according to

the diversity of their faults. And all the plagues of Egypt were figures of spiritual plagues.

blasphemed. That is, because some sins are the cause of sin, some the punishment of sin, some both; as Isaiah says, "Behold thou art wroth, and we have sinned." In this place "to blaspheme God, because of the hail," is acknowledged to be both sin, and the punishment of sin.

ON CHAPTER 17

v. 1. Come. The multitude of the lost which left the Creator, and prostituted itself to commit adultery with demons, is spoken of as sitting upon the waves, that is, the discord of the peoples. But on the contrary, "of the multitude of the believers there was one heart and one soul," whom the Apostle "espoused to one husband, to present them a pure virgin to Christm."

2. kings. The whole is superior to its parts. For the king and inhabitants of the earth are all those who seek proudly for earthly things, whom through the lust of vices, the allurement of the world defiles, and madness of the mind makes drunk.

3. wilderness. By the wilderness, he represents the absence of Deity, Whose presence is paradise.

scarlet beast. The devil, through ungodliness, blood-stained, blasphemous, inflated with the arrogance of presumption, extols the corruption of the wicked.

seven. That is, which has both the kings and kingdoms of the world, whose glory he also shewed to the Lord upon the mountain. For as we said before, universality is often indicated both by the number seven, and the number ten.

4. purple. In purple is shewn the false appearance of simulated rule, in scarlet the blood-stained dress of ungodliness.

gilded. That is, with all the allurements of simulated truth. Lastly, he explains what is within this beauteousness, as follows.

cup. The golden cup full of abominations is hypocrisy, because hypocrites "outwardly appear righteous unto men, but within are full of all uncleanness."

5. forehead. This corrupter at once on her very countenance is shewn to be the nurse of vices. But because she is only discerned by wisdom and prudence, especially under precious ornament, it is indicated that this is a mystical name.

6. saints. There is one body adverse within and without, and although it may seem separate in place, yet it acts in common by unity of spirit. So the

ancestors of the wicked are in sense accused of stoning Zacharias, though they did it not themselves.

8. was, and is not. That is to say, the devil aforetime ruled in the world, and when the Lord was crucified, he was cast out. But at the end of the world he is loosed from the stronghold of his prison, and by the breath of the Lord's mouth will perish for ever. Tichonius refers the beast to the whole body of the devil, which is made up by the course of generations, as they pass away and succeed each other; for this reason above others, that he shews the woman sitting upon the beast, whom he had promised to shew sitting upon the waters, that is, the peoples.

9. heads. The heads of the beast, he says, are the kings of the world, who through the swelling of pride are said to be like exceeding high mountains, on whom there rests a wanton ungodliness, so that they both oppress by violence, and deceive by fraud.

10. five. Seeing that he had described in the number seven the fulness of worldly dominion, the last part of which, that is, the kingdom of Antichrist, had not yet come; he now accordingly testifies that five kings had passed away, that the sixth was present, that the seventh was to come.

short space. Because the Lord beholds us both proud and weak, he says, that the days which he has introduced as singularly evil, are mercifully shortened; in truth, that he may both alarm their pride by the adversity of the time, and refresh their weakness by the shortness of it.

11. eighth. Antichrist, who is to reign at the end of the age, because of the unity of the body of the ungodly of which he is the head, pertains to the number of the kingdoms of the world. But because of his singular power of wickedness, he is also retained in the order of his own proper place.

12. horns. The kingdoms of the world have not yet fully displayed their power in persecuting the Church. For although these even now have rule over the greatest part, yet there will be the stronger power of insane boasting when they have also deceived such by signs. Some understand it, that when the last persecution draws near, there will be ten kings who are to divide the world between, them; according to the prophecy of Daniel also, who said of the fourth beast, "And he had ten horns; and behold another little horn came up from the midst of them, and three of the first horns were plucked up before his face;" and that Antichrist who should arise from Babylon, should subdue the king of Egypt, and of Africa, and that after they were slain, seven other kings should also submit their necks to the conqueror. But others say that Antichrist is placed in the number eleven, to signify prevarication. For eleven indicates a departure from the perfection of the number ten.

as kings. He says, "as kings," because they only reign as in a dream, who oppose the kingdom of Christ.

13. mind. That is, with like consent they make war for the devil with all their will. For this is to receive a kingdom after the beast, by imitating the devil to be adversaries of Christ.

14. overcome. That the weakness of man might not fear the cruelty of the old enemy, he describes the beast which has seven heads, and is armed with the horns of a secular kingdom, as vanquished by Christ triumphant: and then, to denote that He is triumphant in His own, he has added the following.

chosen. He has well premised chosen, for "many are called, but few chosen."

16. hate. They will begin to hate with extreme abhorrence the glory of the world, which they now embrace with wanton love, when at the end they see, now that the Lamb is conqueror, that they themselves are to be condemned. It may also be otherwise understood, either that there are always contentions among the proud; or, that every one "who loves iniquity hates his own soul."

desolate. For they make the world waste through the wrath of God, while they are given up to it, and use it unrighteously.

flesh. When she is deprived of her accustomed delights, they will burn her in the fires of hell.

17. hearts. God, the Judge, he says, just and mighty, and to Whom justice is always pleasing, for the punishment of their former sins suffered the ungodly to do such things, for whose sake He might with reason bring to an end the whole world; as the Gospels testify to have been done in the instance of Sodom, and of the flood.

give. That is, that they should obey the devil until the Scriptures should be fulfilled, in which God said, that in the time of the fourth kingdom He would bring the earth to its consummation; as we read in Daniel, "There shall be the fourth kingdom upon the earth, which shall be more powerful than all these kingdoms, and shall devour, and overthrow, and destroy the whole earthy."

18. city. So also below, when he was bidden to behold the Lamb's wife, he saw the holy city coming down from heaven; and when he described it, he said, "And the kings of the earth shall bring their glory into it." For there are two cities in the world, the one proceeding from the abyss, the other from heaven. And therefore he now compares the same ungodliness, which he had described under the appearance of a harlot naked and burned up, with the ruins of a deserted city.

ON CHAPTER 18

v. 1. another angel. This angel, who is mighty and lightens the earth, may be understood to be as well the Lord Himself incarnate, as the doctors of the Church, who are endued with heavenly light, and announce the end of the world, saying, "The kingdom of heaven is at hand."

2. fallen. O Jerusalem, he says, fear thou not the power of the earthly city, which falls spiritually by the very thing in which it prevails over thee, through the hostility of unholy citizens. Isaiah also describes Babylon as "an habitation of unclean monsters." For it is no other than the city of the devil which receives every unclean spirit, in which all the uncleanness throughout the world abides.

3. rich. He calls those rich in sins, who by an infelicitous traffic exchange their souls for temporal abundance. For excess of luxuries makes poor instead of rich.

4. Come out. So also Isaiah says, "Come out of the midst of them, and touch no unclean thing. Be ye clean who bear the vessels of the Lord." When the fall of Babylon is foretold, he brings in the departure, which is the fall of Babylon. For when Lot has departed from Sodom, it will be utterly destroyed.

6. render. It is from the Church that plagues, both visible and invisible, go forth into the world.

double. In order that she who enjoyed temporal delights may be racked with eternal torments.

7. queen. Because, amid the delights of present luxuries she was unwilling to guard against future vengeance, therefore in a short time will she be punished with destruction, both of the spirit and of the flesh. But, on the contrary, the citizens of the heavenly country, who "set before them Jerusalem as the beginning of their joy, will not sing the Lord's song in a strange land;" that is, they will not entertain at the present time the joy which belongs to the age to come.

9. bewail. This wailing of the kings, and merchants, and sailors of Babylon, may be understood in two ways. It may either be, when, at the day of judgment, all the glory of the world is perishing, and there remains to the ungodly only the presence of their past life, and they say, "What has pride profited us? or what has the vaunting of riches brought us? All these things are passed away as a shadow;" or, when, in the present time, as the abundance of things ceases, and the breaking in pieces of divers nations is at hand, the occasion of carnal delights, ever present for the fulfilment of the desires of the wicked, shall have been taken away.

smoke. This is the indication of perdition, because fire is preceded by smoke. For what else is the confusion and breaking in pieces of the world, than the smoke of a present hell.

10. afar. They stand afar off, not in body, but in mind, while each one fears for himself that which he sees another suffer, through calumny and power.

Babylon. The Spirit mentions the name of the city. But they lament for the world, for that it is overtaken with punishment in so short a time, and all its industry is ruined and made to cease.

11. merchants. They lament that all the pomps of the world, and whatsoever is either pleasant to the bodily senses, or suited to external uses, fails. For the different kinds of metals appertain to the sight, the odours to the smell, the unguents to the touch, the wine, wheat, and oil, to the taste. Moreover, under the name of "beasts and of slaves," they complain that all other aids to humanity perish; and that in a twofold manner, as I said, either because they fail, on the death of the world, or, because the miserable survivors of those who have left the joys of the world through death, mourn, as it were, over the ruins of their city; and who therefore through fear of a similar punishment, are said "to stand afar off."

15. made rich. Wherever the Spirit saith, "made rich by her," He signifies the riches of transgressions. Below, where the voice of the unrighteous is of those who say, "Alas, alas, that great city, wherein all those who have ships in the sea were made rich," material riches are understood. For they think that they were made rich by the craftiness of their own faction.

16. linen. Is the city clothed with fine linen, or with purple, and not with men? Well, it is they who lament for themselves, while they are spoiled of the things which are mentioned above.

17. sailors. Will all they who sail on the sea be able to be present to see the burning of the city? Rather he means, that all the husbandmen and artificers of the age fear for themselves, when they see the ruin of their hope.

18. like this. That is, that the world cannot be restored anew.

19. dust That is. As defaming the face of their leaders, through whom they were reduced and perished; or, as accusing the madness of their own heart, which is the chief part of man, with a too late repentance.

desolate. Observe that every single person of those who lament, weeps not only for the loss of riches, but for the sudden and unforeseen ruin of the deceitful world.

20. rejoice. So also the Lord in the Gospel, when predicting the ruin of the world, added, "When ye shall see these things come to pass, look up and lift up your heads;" that is, make your hearts glad.

avenged. This is the judgment which the souls of the saints sought with the great cry, "How long, O Lord God, holy and true, dost Thou not avenge our blood?"

21. sea. He said, "With this violence shall Babylon be cast;" or, as another version has it, "Thus with violence shall Babylon, the great city, be thrown down." The city of the age, because of the weight and transgression of sins, is compared with an unstable mass. For "the ungodly walk round about." And justly is it swallowed up by the waves of vengeance, because it overwhelmed the city of Jerusalem with the waves of unbelief, when, as they sat by the streams of Babylon, they bewailed their absence from the heavenly Sion. So the Lord says, "that they who cause offence," shall be visited with a similar punishment. And the Church, indeed, is represented as like a stone, but one that is stable and firm, which despises the assaults of the tempests. The mass may also be understood of the breaking to pieces by punishments. For so the blessed Ignatius, when about to suffer, is reported to have said, "I am the corn of God, I shall be ground by the teeth of beasts, that I may be made a pure loaf."

22. voice. Of the five senses he had deferred sound, which he now says is taken away from the world among other things. As if he said, that which is beautiful to see, melodious to hear, smooth to touch, sweet to smell, delicious to taste, is to pass away from the world.

craftsman. All things, he says, which appertain to the use or pleasure of human life, are taken from the ungodly; and he has added the reason in that which follows.

23. great men. That is, because "in life thou receivedst thy good things."

24. prophets. Did the same city kill the Apostles, which also killed the prophets, or all the saints? Rather is this the city which Cain founded in the blood of his brother, and called by the name of his son Enoch, that is, of all his posterity, as seven generations of Cain are described. For the building or that city, then, is shed "all the righteous blood, from the blood of righteous Abel unto the blood of Zacharias," that is, of people and priest.

ON CHAPTER 19

v. 1. trumpets (multitudes). These things the Church now says in part, but will say perfectly when the separation has taken place, and when it has been more openly avenged.

2. corrupted. He relates two actions of the harlot, namely, that she corrupted herself with the bad, and persecuted the good; and in these two, I suppose, he comprehends all the crimes of the wicked.

3. Alleluia. The Church extols the Lord for His judgments with unceasing love. For Alleluia signifies, "Praise ye the Lord." Lastly, the Psalms which have for the beginning, "Praise ye the Lord," begin in the Hebrew with Alleluia.

rises up. "Rises up," he says, not "will rise up." But Babylon always goes into perdition, and is in part already burning, while Jerusalem passes into paradise, as the Lord manifests in the poor man and the rich.

4. worshipped. The Church worships God, not with the service of the lips alone, but with the sweetness of the highest devotion.

Amen; Alleluia. Although these words can be interpreted, for they are translated, as I said, "to the faith," or "truth," and "praise of the Lord," yet in reverence for their sacredness the authority of the original language is preserved to them. For the Church also continually sings Alleluia on the Lord's day, and the whole period of the fifty days, because of the hope of the resurrection, which is to be in praise of the Lord.

5. Praise ye. Seeing he commands this to be done, and mentions that it was done, he indicates, that the praise of the elect servants was approved. "Small," he says, "and great," for slightness of understanding does not harm, where heart and tongue are filled with the praise of the Lord.

6. trumpet. (multitude.) Great is the voice of those who sing, great the devotion of heart. For with a manifold repetition of praise it celebrates at once the fall of the ungodly, and the eternal glory of the Lord and His own.

7 marriage. It is the marriage of the Lamb, when the Church is to be united unto the Lord in the marriage-chamber of the heavenly kingdom.

ready. By always insisting on works of righteousness, she has shewn herself worthy of the spiritual feast and the everlasting kingdom. It may also be taken in accordance with the parable of the Gospel, which relates, that on the bridegroom's coming, "the virgins arise and trim their lamps," that is, reckon with themselves their works, for which they expect to receive eternal blessedness.

8. arrayed. It was given to her to be arrayed in her own deeds. But on the contrary, they who according to Isaiah "weave a spider's web," will not be clothed with their own works. For their works are unprofitable works.

9. supper. He relates that they are called not to dinner, but to supper, because assuredly the banquet at the end of the day is a supper. Accordingly, they who come to the refection of heavenly contemplation, when the time of the present life is ended, are called to the marriage-supper of the Lamb.

true. That is, the things will assuredly come to pass which I have announced as future.

10. fellowservant. He had said above, "I am the first and the last." He shews, therefore, that the angel was sent as a figure of the Lord and the Church. In the same manner he also says at the end, "I, Jesus, have sent my angel to testify these things to you in the churches."

testimony. After that the Lord Jesus Christ raised the person of man, which He assumed, above the heavens, the angel feared to be worshipped by man, namely, as worshipping the God-man above himself. Yet we read of this having been done before the Incarnation of the Lord by men, and not in any wise forbidden by the angels.

prophecy. For whatever the Spirit of prophecy said, is the testimony of Jesus, Who receives testimony from the law and the prophets. Do not thou, then, worship me, he says, as God, seeing that I have come to bear testimony to His powers. Thus far concerning the fall of Babylon, henceforth concerning the future glory of Jerusalem.

11. White. The Lord, "Who is the way, the truth, and the life.," and to Whom it is said by the prophet, "Because thou hast wrought wonderful things, the faithful counsels of old, Amen," ascends upon a white, that is, an immaculate body, to vanquish the powers of the air.

judge. He judges, as the King of ages. He makes war, because in His members He Himself of His compassion always contends.

12 eyes. He sometimes calls the precepts, sometimes the Spirit, the eyes of the Lord. He says, "Thy word, O Lord, is a lantern unto my feet," and of the Spirit, "I have come to send a fire upon the earth."

diadems, (crowns). In Him, in Whom we shall do mighty things, the multitude of the saints is said to have the ornament of a crown.

name. "No one knows but He Himself," he says, because all the Church is in Him. For the perfect knowledge of the Word of God is manifested to those who have obtained to be the body of Christ and His members. In the same manner the Lord says, "No one has ascended up to heaven, but He Who descended from heaven, the Son of Man, Who is in heaven."

13. vesture. The vesture of Christ ought to be understood according to the place. Here, accordingly, it appears to indicate the very act of the Passion, so that in the white horse is designated the immaculate birth, in the vesture stained with blood, the innocent death.

The Word. Because the same Who appeared for a time as a man of suffering, "in the beginning was God with God." He is called the Word, because nothing in His nature was visible, nor corporeal; or, because the Father made all things by Him, the perfect knowledge of Whose nature, as he says above, is known to Himself alone, and to the Father. For, "the peace of God passeth all understanding;" that is, the peace by which God Himself was reconciled unto Himself, exceeds the wisdom of any creature, whether human or angelic, for "Of his wisdom there is no number." For when it is said, "And he, to whom the Son will reveal," that is, the Father and the Son, "knows," this has respect to the capacity of the creature.

14. armies. That is to say, the Church in white bodies imitated Him. For because of the intensity of its conflict, it rightly receives the name of an army.

linen. This he himself explained above to be "the righteousness of saints;" as it is said by the Psalmist, "Let thy priests be clothed with righteousness."

15. sword. So also Isaiah says, "And he hath set my mouth as a sharp sword;" and the Apostle, "And the sword of the Spirit, which is the Word of God."

winepress. It is even so. For now also He treads until He tread without the city.

16. Name. This is the Name, which no one of the proud knows. But it is written on the Church, "not with ink, but by the Spirit of the living God," that is to say, "on the tables of the heart." For by the thigh is designated the posterity of seed. Therefore Abraham also, in order that his posterity might not be mixed with aliens, made use of his thigh for a third testimony between himself and his servant. And of this also the Apostle, as it were raising up seed to a brother who has died, says, "In Christ Jesus I have begotten you through the Gospel." It may also be understood, that the Church by serving reigns in Christ, and has lordship over lords. The same Name is also inscribed on the vesture, because by the mystery of the Nativity, and the act of the Passion, His majesty and kingdom are revealed to us. In that which follows, he explains

what the appearance of the King and of the army signifies, namely, the glory of the last conflict, and of the kingdom which succeeds to it.

17. sun. That is, preaching in the Church, which shines the more brightly, and thunders forth the more freely, the more it is oppressed.

birds. He calls the saints birds, as passing their life in heaven. For "wheresoever the body is, there will the eagles be gathered together;" and as bringing them together into one body, he had said, "flying in the midst of heaven;"

Come. Come, he says, ye who hunger and thirst after righteousness, to the banquet of the kingdom to come, when, the fierceness of the proud repressed, ye shall be satisfied with the light of divine justice.

18. sit. I suppose that these are the horsemen whom, at the opening of the seals, he had described as having come against the white horse of the Lord.

19. beast. He explains in what manner the supper of the Lord was prepared, namely, in that the devil fought against the Church, and was vanquished.

20. both. He appears to signify, that the devil and Antichrist are to be visited with so much greater a punishment than the rest of men and demons, as it is more grievous to be burned alive with flames of brimstone, than to die quickly, and be slain with the stroke of a sword; unless, perhaps, he intends that the divine attention was directed to them first. For "he who does not believe is already judged;" whether thou understand Antichrist to be intended by the false prophet, or heretics, for not one of mortal men sins more obstinately than heretics, who after they have known Christ, deny Him.

21. filled. "If the righteous shall even now rejoice when he seeth the vengeance" upon the wicked, how much more then, when in the presence of the Judge Himself, he will be made one spirit with Him. The birds may also be understood to be evil spirits, who will be satiated from their destruction. Tichonius expounds this supper as follows: "In all time the Church devours the flesh of its enemies, while it is devoured by them. But in the resurrection it will be satiated, as avenged for their carnal work.

ON CHAPTER 20

v. 1. abyss. He recapitulates from the beginning, and more fully, in what way he had said above, "The beast which thou sawest was, and is not; and is to ascend from the abyss, and will go into perdition." The Lord, therefore, endued with His Father's power, descends and is incarnate, to wage war with the prince of the world, and when he is bound to spoil his goods.

2. devil. "Diabolus," is interpreted, "flowing downward." But in Greek he is called "the accuser." "Satan is "the adversary," or "prevaricator." So he is called "the dragon," on account of his malice in hurting; "the serpent," on account of cunning in deceiving; "the devil," on account of the fall of his estate; "Satan," on account of obstinacy in opposition against the Lord.

bound him. That is, he kept back and restrained his power from seducing men who were to be set free. For if he were permitted to exert the whole of this, either by force, or deceit, he would beguile most of the weak in so long a time. By the "thousand years," he intended a part, namely, the remainder of the thousand years of the sixth day, in which the Lord was born and suffered.

3. cast. He cast him, that is, into the hearts of the persecuting people. Not that the devil was not there before; when he was sent forth from believers, he began to possess the ungodly, who are not only alienated from God, but who hate more grievously those who serve God. And this the Lord openly shewed, when He sent him forth from men into the swine.

seal. He interdicted him, and as by a royal seal prevented him from seducing the nations; namely those which were appointed unto life, which he seduced before, that they should not be reconciled to God.

loosed. "Then," as St. Augustine says, "he will be loosed, when also the time will be short. For, as we read, he will rage three years and a-half with all his own powers, and the powers of his own, and they with whom he will make war will be such, that his violence and wiles, great as they are, will not be able to overcome them. But if he was never loosed, his malignant power would the less appear, the most faithful patience of the holy city the less be proved, the less finally would it be discerned, how well the Almighty God made use of his great evil."

4. judgment. He indicates that which is done in the thousand years in which Satan is bound. For the Church, which in Christ will sit on twelve thrones to judge, now sits and judges, seeing that she has obtained to hear from her King, "whatsoever thou shalt bind on earth shall be bound in heaven."

souls. That which he is to say afterwards is understood, "they reigned with Christ a thousand years." The Church therefore reigns with Christ in the living and in the dead. For "to this end," as the Apostle says, "Christ died, that He might be Lord both of the living and the dead;" and for this reason he has mentioned the souls of the martyrs alone, that they chiefly reign after death, who even unto death have contended for the truth.

worshipped. We ought to understand this both of the living and of the dead. For they who are still alive in this mortal flesh, as well as they who are departed, even now reign with Christ, through all the interval which is signified by the number of a thousand years, in a certain manner which is congruous with this present time.

5. the rest. Whosoever have not heard the voice of the Son of God, and passed to life from death, during all that time in which the first resurrection takes place, that is, the resurrection of souls, in the second resurrection, which is the resurrection of the flesh, will assuredly pass with the flesh itself into the second death, that is, into eternal torments.

first resurrection. That certainly is the first resurrection in which we rise again through baptism, as the Apostle says, "If ye have risen with Christ, seek the things which are above." For as the first death in this life is through sins, since "the soul that sinneth, it shall die," so also the first resurrection is in this life through remission of sins.

6. Blessed. That is, he who has kept the state of being born again.

saints. Another version has "priests of God and of Christ," and it is not said of bishops only and of presbyters, who properly are called "priests" in the Church. But as we are all called Christs because of the mystical chrism, so are we all called priests, because we are members of the one Priest, of Whom the Apostle Peter says, "a holy people, a royal priesthood."

reign. The Spirit when He wrote this, declared that the Church would reign a thousand years, that is, unto the end of the world; and a doubt might arise from this. For that it is concerning a perpetual kingdom is manifest.

7. finished. By "finished" he intended a part by the whole. For he will be loosed in such a manner that there will remain the three years and six months

of the last conflict. But apart from this figure, the time is rightly said to be ended. For so small a remnant is not to be taken into account, when seven hundred years, and as many as God wills, are called by the Apostle "an hour.

8. seduce. He will then seduce them, to the end that he may gather them together to this battle. For even before he used to seduce them in whatever manner he was able, through many different evils. And "he will go out" means, he will burst forth into open persecution from the hiding-places of his hatred. Moreover, Gog and Magog either denote the whole by a part, or according to the interpretation of the names, which signify "a roof" and "from a roof," "they indicate secret and open enemies. For they themselves are both "a roof," because the enemy is now shut up in them, and ruled, and they will also be "from a roof," when they shall burst forth into open hatred.

9. breadth. They certainly are not represented as having come, or as about to come, to one place, as if the beloved city, that is, the Church, were to be confined within some one place. For much rather wished he to intimate by "the breadth of the earth," that it would be persecuted in all nations; and by the term "camp," that not even then would it forsake its warfare.

fire. It must not be supposed that this is the final punishment But it is rather the fire of envy, with which the adversary will be tormented through the firmness of the saints. For "heaven" is the firmament. This is the fire which went forth from the mouth of the witnesses of God, and it will devour their enemies. For in the last day He will not rain fire upon them, but when they have been gathered together before Him and judged, He will send them into eternal fire, concerning which it is here added, as follows.

10. cast. That is, at the last judgment the devil will be cast into eternal fire, where also are all those whom he sent before him, that is, the greatest part of the ungodly city, inasmuch as the beast is to be taken according to the place, sometimes as the devil, sometimes as Antichrist, sometimes as the ungodly city itself. But under the name of "fire coming down from heaven," may also be designated the sudden destruction of the ungodly, when the Lord at His coming will slay Antichrist with the breath of His mouth. He explains more fully how, when Christ is Judge, the devil with his own is cast into the fire.

11. throne. He said that he "saw Him sitting on the throne, from Whose sight the heaven and the earth fled away." For after the judgment is ended, the heaven and the earth cease to be, when there begin to be a new heaven and a new earth; that is, by the change of the things that are, and not by any means by their destruction. For "the fashion of this world passeth away." He said not also the substance, in that we believe that the same is to be changed for the better.

12. stand. "When the Son of Man shall sit on the throne of His glory, then will be gathered before Him all nations."

book of life. Another version has, "which is of the life of each one." So then by "the opened books," he means the Testaments of God, for the world will be judged according to both Testaments. By "the book of the life of each one," he means the memory of our actions, and not that the discerner of hidden things has a memorial book.

written. That is to say, they were judged out of the Testaments, namely, according to that they did from them or did not. The hooks may also be understood to be the deeds of the righteous. For while the reprobate are condemned by comparison with these, in the spreading out of these they read, as it were, the good which they themselves were unwilling to do.

13. sea. This, without doubt, took place before that the dead were judged. Having, therefore, recapitulated that which he had passed over, he pursues the order of things.

14. death and Hades. So he signifies that the bodies are to be gathered from the earth, and the souls from their own places. For by the name of "death" he designates good souls, which have only suffered the dissolution of the flesh, and not punishment too; and by the term Hades, bad. And it may also be taken literally, that all the bodies, even those which the deep has swallowed, or the wild beast has devoured, will rise again. And Tichonius expounds it thus: "The people which he will here find alive are the dead of the sea, 'And death and Hades gave up their dead.' These are the people which are buried. But when he had said, that 'they were judged, every one according to works,' he briefly subjoined, that "both death and Hades were cast into the lake of fire.' He means the devil and his own, whom Hades followed above, as he sat on the pale horse. So he repeats what he had already said more plainly by anticipation, 'And the devil who seduced them, was cast into the lake of fire and brimstone.' But that which he had added above more obscurely concerning the beast and the false prophet, he here more openly sets forth.

15. found written. That is, who was not judged by God to be alive. And so they appear to me to speak more correctly, who interpret the opened books above to be the consciences and works of each one; and the book of life the fore-knowledge of God, which cannot be deceived, concerning those to whom eternal life will be given, in which they are written, that is, foreknown. As the judgment is ended in which he saw the bad to be condemned, it remains that he also speak concerning the good.

ON CHAPTER 21

v. 1. new. This is the order in which that will take place which he has already spoken of by anticipation, that he "saw one sitting on the throne, from whose face the heaven and the earth fled away;" namely, when the ungodly were judged. Then the fashion of this world will pass away by the conflagration of the supernal fires, that when the heaven and the earth are changed for the better, the incorruption and immortality of holy bodies may have a condition of existence corresponding with the twofold change.

sea. As to what he here says, whether it is dried up in that extreme heat, or whether it also is changed for the better, I could not easily say. For we read of "a new heaven and a new earth" as future, but not also of a new sea. But as it is not unusual in prophetical language to intermix metaphysical with proper terms, it may perhaps be, that he has represented the turbulent life of this age, which will then come to an end, under the name of the sea

2. new Jerusalem. This city is said to "come down from heaven," for that God made it by heavenly grace.

adorned. For there is another Jerusalem which is not adorned for her husband, but for an adulterer.

3. people. God Himself will be to the elect the reward of eternal blessedness, which, as possessed by Him, they will possess for ever.

4. tears. So great and so exalted will the glory of that city appear from the gift of God, as that there remain in it no vestiges of old age, since both a heavenly incorruption will refine their bodies, and the sight of the eternal King will feed their mind.

death. For he had said that death was cast into the lake of fire. For the same sentence may also be understood thus, that when the holy city is glorified at the last judgment, pain, grief, and mortality only remain in hell.

6. write. These things it behoves to be believed, not explained, especially because he says, that "it is done" of the past, so as not to suffer any one to doubt of the future.

Omega. As He testified at the beginning of the book that He was this, so it had need to be repeated the third time, that "neither before Him," as Isaiah says, "nor after Him," should there be believed to be another. And because the discourse is of the end of the world, the finisher of the age Himself, Who is called the Creator, may be understood.

athirst. He now sprinkles believers in the way from the fountain, which, in their own country, He grants to those who overcome to be abundantly drawn forth. And both are a free gift. For "the gift of God is eternal life in Christ Jesus our Lord," and "of His fulness have we all received, and grace for grace."

8. fearful. To introduce a caution, he always mingles with the bland the austere. So also the hundred-and-forty-fourth Psalm, when making known abundantly the grace of the Lord's mercies, suddenly brings in His severe judgment, saying, "The Lord preserveth all them that love Him, and all sinners will He destroy." And he joins the fearful with the unbelieving, because he fears to incur the danger of the contest, who doubts of the reward of the conqueror.

liars. He shews that there are many kinds of lying, but that the most dangerous and most detestable is that in which there is sin against religion, concerning which he says above, "They say that they are Jews, and are not, but they lie, for they are the synagogue of Satan."

9. seven. The same preachers who inflict the sevenfold, that is, the universal plague upon the ungodly, reveal also to the Church the joys that are to come.

bride. He calls the Church the "bride" and "wife," in that it remains immaculate, and always brings forth spiritual sons to God. Or, this is because she is now betrothed to God, and is then to be brought to an immortal marriage.

10. mountain. After the fall of Babylon, the holy city, which is the bride of the Lamb, is seen placed on a mountain. For the stone "cut out from the mountain without hands," broke in pieces the image of worldly glory, and became a great mountain, and filled the whole world.

11. glory. For she will then appear more beautiful, when through the Spirit by Whom her husband is believed to have been conceived and born, she has attained to bear fully the heavenly image.

precious. The precious stone is Christ, Who says, "The glory which Thou gavest Me, I have given them."

jasper. It is compared with jasper from the whiteness of virtues; to crystal, from the inner purity of the mind, and faith unfeigned.

12. wall. That is, the impregnable firmness of faith, hope, and love. The Lord also Himself Who protects the Church on every side, may be understood to be the wall, of Whom also Isaiah says, "There shall be placed in her a wall

and bulwark;" that is, the protection of the Lord, and the intercession of the saints, who make a way for Him by teaching to the heart of believers.

gates. These gates are the Apostles, who primarily, either by writing, or by work, laid open to all nations an entrance into the Church.

angels. These are doctors, who follow the footsteps of the Apostles in the mystery of the faith and word.

names. He signifies the memory of the ancient fathers implanted in the hearts of preachers. And so also the high-priest, when about to enter the tabernacle, was commanded to bear the memorial of the fathers upon the breastplate of judgment.

13. east. By this so elaborate description of the gates, he wished, I suppose, to indicate the mystery of the number twelve, by which, accordingly, either the sum of the Apostles, or the perfection of the Church, may be represented; for that the faith of the Holy Trinity was to be made known by it to the foursquare world.

14. foundations. That which the gates are, the same are the foundations; that which the city is, the same are the walls. But the patriarchs may also be signified by the term "foundations," in that they contained within themselves the names, that is, the figure of the Apostles. For by them, as foundations, although by the Apostles, as by gates, this city has been opened to the nations which shall believe. And it is to be noted, that "the foundations," when they are spoken of in the plural, signify the doctors, or virtues, of the Church; but when in the singular, the Lord Himself, Who is the foundation of foundations.

15. measure. Christ, Who is the "wisdom of God," "reaching from one end to another mightily, and ordering all things sweetly," measures the holy city. For, "ordering all things in number and measure and weight," He distributes to each one of the faithful the gifts of spiritual graces. The doctors of the Church may also be understood, in that with frail bodies, but heavenly minds, they carefully examine the deserts of every one.

16. foursquare. The city is therefore said to be set in a square, and to be placed of an equal dimension on every side, in that it is not suffered to be marked by any inequality. For "to be perfect," as the Apostle says, that is, "to be wise, to have peace," is truly to subsist in the solidity of a square.

furlongs. That is, He beheld the Church, or gave her to be, perfect in faith and deeds. For the perfection of the four principal virtues, exalted by the faith of the Holy Trinity, composes as by the number ten the dignity of the Church.

equal. This is the solidity of invincible truth, by which the Church is not suffered to be "carried about by every wind of doctrine," as resting upon the length of faith, the breadth of love, the height of hope. And if it has but one the less of these, there will not be the perfect stability of the Church.

17. an hundred and forty-four. This sum contains the square of the number twelve, for twelve times twelve are an hundred and forty-four, and itself also signifies the perfection of the holy city.

a man. The Church exists, as chosen from among men, and as exalted by the promises of Christ it hopes for an equality with angels. But literally he signifies, that the angel appeared to him in the form of a man.

18. building. This is the same with the exhortation of the Apostle Peter, "and be ye, as spiritual stones, built upon spiritual houses."

glass. The Church is represented by gold, since it is often described as adorned with golden candle-sticks and bowls, because of the attire of wisdom. But he refers the glass to a belief of the truth. For the same that appears without is also within, and there is nothing simulated, and which is not perspicuous, in the saints of the Church. It may also be referred to the time when the thoughts of all towards each other are perspicuous and declared.

19. precious stones. By the names of the several stones is shewn either the form, or the order, or the variety of the virtues, of which the whole heavenly Jerusalem is built up. For it is a difficult thing for each one singly to flourish in all virtues. Finally, Isaiah, in describing the adornment of the same city when he said, "Behold I will lay thy stones in order, and lay thy foundations in sapphires," and the rest, immediately subjoined, as if in explanation, "All thy children taught of the Lord."

jasper. here are many kinds of jaspers. For one appears of a green colour, and marked, as it were, with flowers. Another resembles an emerald, but is of an opaque colour, and it is supposed that all phantasms are put to flight by it. Another is glistering, as of a mixed colour, with snow and the foam of sea waves. By the jasper, therefore, is shewn the unfading verdure of faith, which is imbued with the sacrament of the Lord's Passion by the water of Baptism, and is prepared by increasing deserts for all the flowers of spiritual graces. And he who has this puts to flight vain fears, as the blessed Peter admonishes, "Your adversary the devil goeth about as a roaring lion, seeking whom he may devour, whom resist stedfast in the faith;" and he is able to say with the spouse, "My beloved is white and ruddy." Therefore with good reason in Isaiah also, the bulwarks of the same city are alike fortified and adorned by this stone and structure of the wall.

sapphire. Moses set forth alike the colour and the sacrament of this stone, when in describing the appearance of God he said, "Under His feet, as it were, a work of a sapphire stone, and as the heaven when it is clear." Ezekiel also says, that the place in which the throne of God is, "has the likeness of a sapphire," and that the glory of the Lord consists of this colour, which bears the image of the super-celestial; so that he who is such, is able to say with the Apostle, "But our conversation is in heaven;" and when struck by the rays of the sun, emits a radiant brightness from himself; because the mind of the saints, which is always intent on heavenly things, in that it is daily renewed by the rays of divine light, with more compunction in some sort, and more fervency, diligently seeks for the things eternal, and commends them to others for their seeking. For that it is said to be found in the Red Sea signifies, that by the Passion of the Lord, and the laver of holy Baptism, the minds of mortal men are raised on high, to anticipate the things of heaven.

chalcedony. The chalcedony shines with a pale light, as of the flame of a lamp, and has its brilliancy in the open air, and not in the house. And by it are described those who rest upon a heavenly desire, and yet escape the notice of men, and who practise as in a secret place their fasting, and alms, and prayers; but when they are bidden to go forth for teaching, or other necessities of the saints, shew presently how much brilliancy they have borne within. For that which is said to resist cutting, but to attract bits of chaff if it is struck by the rays of the sun, or is heated by the rubbing of the fingers, deservedly corresponds with those who do not allow their fortitude to be overcome by another; but rather themselves make the weak attain to the privileges of their own light and ardour. And of one of them it is said, "he was a burning and a shining lamp," burning, that is, in love, shining in discourse. For they always rekindle the light of their virtues with the oil of internal charity, that it may not fail. And that it is produced among the Nasamones, who form a province of Ethiopia, indicates that these under the ardent fervour of love, yet with obscure fame, as with a black skin, are accounted vile.

emerald. The emerald is of so exceedingly deep a green as to surpass all the green herbs, leaves, and gems, and it colours green the air reflected round, and it deservedly increases in greenness although naturally imbued with it. And there are very many kinds of this stone, but the most famous are the Scythian; the Bactrian hold the second place, the Egyptian the third. Accordingly, it represents souls always flourishing in faith, which the more they are tried by the opposition of the world, which is denoted by the cold of Scythia, strive the more to conceive in their mind by hope "the unfading and eternal inheritance which is reserved in heaven," and extend it to their neighbours by preaching. And these also by the cup of the Lord's Passion, and the unction of internal charity which is given through the Holy Spirit, advance toward the contempt of the world. With these also the land which is the country of the same stone corresponds in a beautiful manner, a land which is rich but uninhabitable. For although it is plentiful in gold and gems, the whole of it is occupied by griffons, very fierce birds, or rather flying beasts, Since they are fourfooted, and in body indeed are like lions, but in head and wings like eagles. The Arimaspians, who are said to be remarkable for a Single eye in the middle of the forehead, fight with them, that they may obtain these stones, which these creatures seize with wonderful avidity, and the Arimaspians guard. It was to this land, abounding in treasures of virtues, that the Psalmist had gone, when he said, "Behold, I fled away far off, and remained in the wilderness;" that is, by fleeing far off, I withdrew my soul from the allurements of the world. Here he had met with the wild beasts which were opposed to him, when he said, under inspiration, "Let the deceitful lips he made dumb, which speak iniquity against the righteous, in pride and contempt." Here also he shews that he found desirable riches, in that with gladsome admonition he proceeded to add this, "How great is the abundance of Thy sweetness, O Lord, which Thou hast laid up in secret for them that fear Thee," and the rest to the end of the Psalm. Against birds of this kind, which desire greedily to snatch away from us the seed of the divine word, all the saints watch with a single intention through heavenly desire, as if to be admired for one eye; that they may be able to search out and dig up the gem of faith and of all other virtues. For indeed the higher any virtue is, the fewer admirers has it, and the heavier persecution does it endure from unclean spirits, who like horrible griffons, are of the earth in the baseness of their deserts, but of the air in the loftiness of their proud mind; and who strive with unwearied labour not to possess spiritual riches for their own use, but to take them away from men. And because such sublimity of faith has become known to the world through the Gospel, in that there are four books of the Gospel, the emerald is fitly put in the fourth place.

20. sardonyx. This derives its whiteness from the onyx, and redness from the sard, and it has received from the two the name sardonyx. But there are very many kinds of it: for one preserves a likeness to red earth; another appears to be of two colours, as the blood shines through the human nail; another consists of three colours, the lowest black, the middle white, the highest vermillion. And with this are compared men reddened through suffering of the body, white through purity of spirit, but lowly in their own eyes through humility of mind, protesting with the Apostle, "Though our outward man perish, yet our inward man is 'renewed day by day;" and again, "I know nothing against myself, yet am I not hereby justified." And so also the Psalmist says, "Although man walk in the image" of God, that is, from the power of the mind, "yet he will be disquieted in vain," that is, from the weakness of the

flesh. This suffering also is through the weakness of the body, for they "who kill the body are not able to kill the soul;" and humility descends from the frailness of the same body, when it is said, "O wretched man that I am! who shall deliver me from the body of this death?" The sardonyx is rightly placed in the fifth foundation, for it is certain that our body depends on five senses.

a sard. The sard, which is entirely of a blood-red colour, signifies the glory of martyrs, of which it is said, "precious in the sight of the Lord is the death of His saints," and is with reason put in the sixth place, seeing that our Lord was incarnate in the sixth period of the age, and was crucified on the sixth day of the week for the salvation of the whole world.

a chrysolite. The chrysolite shines as if it were gold, with burning sparks. And by the appearance of this stone are represented those who shine through their knowledge of the heavenly wisdom, and who impart to their neighbours the words of exhortation, or even the signs of powers, as sparks of fire. And of these, as Arator says,—

"Their minds with love instinct, their ardent zeal
In words breaks forth."

And because this is accomplished through the gift of spiritual grace alone, the chrysolite is most becomingly in the seventh foundation. For the grace of the Holy Spirit is wont very commonly to be represented by the number seven, as it is said of Him above, "And from the seven spirits which are before the throne." And it is consonant also with this sense, that a certain kind of the same stone is found of an azure green colour, whence also among the Hebrews, from the resemblance to the colour of the sea, it is called Tharsis. For greenness appertains to the integrity of faith, which is called "the beginning of wisdom," but water in a figurative sense to the Holy Spirit, the Lord bearing witness, Who says, "He that believeth on Me, as the Scripture saith, out of his belly shall flow rivers of living water. But this spake He of the Spirit, which they that believe on Him should receive."

beryl. The beryl is as if thou shouldest imagine water to be struck by the rays of the sun, and to give out a ruddy and beautiful colour. But it does not shine unless it is shaped by polishing to an hexangular form. For the reflected brightness of the angles is intensified. But it signifies men who are naturally sagacious in intellect, but who shine the more by the light of heavenly grace. For that water designates the depth of understanding, Solomon is witness, who says, "The words of a man's mouth are as deep water." But neither human, nor indeed divine wisdom is of perfect brilliancy, unless the consummation of works is superadded. For perfection of action is often designated by the number six, especially as in this number the work of the world was consummated.

And in that it is said to burn the hand of one who holds it, this is beyond doubt apparent, that whosoever is united to a holy man is indeed refreshed by the fire of his good conversation.

topaz. As the opportunity is rare for the discovery of this stone, so also is the quantity of the commodity scanty. It is said to have two colours, one of the purest gold, the other shining with ethereal brightness. There is a rosy plumpness, and modest purity. It is close to the chrysoprase in size, or colour, as it is in an especial manner a lamp, when it is struck by the rays of the sun, and surpasses the most precious brilliancy of all gems, and attracts in a singular way the most eager desire of the eyes. And if thou wilt polish it, thou makest it dark; if thou wilt leave it in its own proper nature, it is radiant. This stone is said to be an object of admiration to kings themselves, so that they recognise no possession like it among their riches; and the most beautiful quality of its nature is with the best reason compared with the grace of the contemplative life. For holy kings, "whose heart is in the hand of God," deservedly prefer this to all the riches of good works, and the gems of virtues; and they direct towards it most of all the glance of their pure thought, and their sight; and they embrace in their mind the more ardently the sweetness of the spiritual life, as they more frequently receive in themselves the reflected splendour of supernal grace. Holy men, therefore, have a golden colour from the flame of internal charity; and they have also an ethereal one from the contemplation of supernal sweetness; and this often deteriorates from the whirl of the present age, as from the rubbing of a file. For in one and the same moment the mind cannot easily be tormented by earthly labours, sorrows, cares, and pains, and behold with delight, in the condition of a tranquil mind, the joys of the heavenly life. Yea, rather it proclaims this by its groans; "Mine eye," it says, "is confused, because of anger; I have grown old among all mine enemies." But that it is said to be found in an island, of Thebes, which is named Topazion from whence it has also received its name, is to be understood in two ways; namely, that those regions, that is, of the Egyptians, abound most of all in companies of monks, and that whosoever dwells near the Sun of righteousness is indeed coloured by the brightness of ethereal light. And the gem of contemplative sweetness is beautifully put the ninth in order, as the perfection of active life is the eighth; or, because nine orders of angels, whose life it imitates, are found in holy Scripture; or, because it is removed from the denarius of perfect blessedness by the one step of death. It was for this that the prophet panted with the greatest desire, when he said, "Therefore I have loved Thy commandments above gold and the topaz," that is, I was delighted with the most sweet love of Thy commandments, above all the glory of approved action, and above all the sublimity of contemplative joy, which can come to pass in this age; and "the first and greatest of these is, 'Thou shalt love the Lord thy God, with all thy heart, all thy soul, all thy strength.' " But it is most certain that this can only be brought to perfection in the height of the heavenly kingdom.

chrysoprase. The chrysoprase has a mixture of green and gold, deriving from it a certain purple gleam, with specks of gold interspersed. It is found in India; and it signifies, that they who well deserve the verdure of the eternal country by the brightness of perfect love, make it manifest also to others by the purple light of their own martyrdom. For since they follow the example of the Lord manifest in the flesh, in that they despise the present life, and prefer eternal glory, they shew even now, as if in India, that is, near the rising of the sun, the brightness of their own deserts. And because they desire to "shine as the sun in the kingdom of the Father," and there to reign with their King with Whom they now suffer, and wait for this, they are rightly put in the tenth place. For by the denarius, with which the dressers of the Lord's vineyard are rewarded, is represented the image of the eternal King, which is to be received when, as it could not be in the ninth degree, through the perfect love of God and of our neighbour, the decalogue will in all points be fulfilled.

jacinth. The jacinth is found in Ethiopia, and has an azure colour. The best is that which is neither transparent nor dull from its opacity, but has a clearness from the two qualities, and resembles the sweetly purified flower. It is not always equally glistering, but changes with the face of the sky. For when this is serene, it is clear and pleasing; but when it is cloudy, it pales and becomes dull before the eyes. And it indicates souls which are always given up to heavenly contemplation, and which, in a certain way, and so far as is permitted to mortals, approach the angelical life. These are enjoined, "to preserve the heart with all keeping of observation," lest on the one hand, with too much subtlety of thought, they dare to inquire into things higher and better than themselves. For, "It is the glory of the Lord to conceal a word." And this is to philosophise with caution concerning God, and the Man Christ; or, lest on the other hand, through the torpor of sloth, they fall back on the weak beginnings of faith, and "the first principles of the words of God." Yea, rather let them walk in the pathway of the King, and go on, protected by "the armour of righteousness on the right hand and on the left," and by a fit observance of the time let them change their face with the sky, and say to the beholders, "For whether we be beside ourselves, it is to God; or whether we be sober, it is for you." As a jacinth surrounded by a cloud, he speaks thus, "Ye are not straitened in us, but in your own bowels;" and again, "For I determined not to know anything among you, save Jesus Christ, and Him crucified." And as one seen in a serene light, he says, "But we speak wisdom among those who are perfect."

amethyst. The amethyst is purple, mixed with a violet colour, and as it were the bloom of the rose, and it emits gently certain small flames. But there appears also to be something in its purple, which is not altogether fiery, but like red wine. So, then, the beautiful tint of the purple designates the condition of the heavenly kingdom, but that of the rose and violet, the lowly modesty and precious death of the saints, namely, in that their mind indeed is chiefly raised on high, even when they are seen outwardly to endure what is vile. For in adversity they are ever mindful of the promise of the Lord," Fear not, little flock, for it is your Father's good pleasure to give you the kingdom." And they not only extend the flame of love to one another, but also to their persecutors themselves. And on their knees they implore, "Lord, lay not this sin to their charge." Moreover, while they drink the cup of passion, they are inebriated instead with the remembrance of the wine "which makes glad the heart of man," of which the Lord promised, that He would drink it new with them in His Father's kingdom."

In the jasper, therefore, is, represented the verdure of faith; in the sapphire the light of heavenly hope; in the chalcedony the flame of internal charity. Again, in the emerald is expressed the bold confession of the same faith in the midst of opposition; in the sardonyx, the humility of the saints amid their virtues; in the sard, the revered blood of martyrs. So in the chrysolyte is shewn spiritual preaching in the midst of miracles; in the beryl, the perfect work of preachers; in the topaz, their fervent contemplation. Moreover, in the chrysoprase are designated at once the work and the reward of the blessed martyrs; in the jacinth, the heavenly exaltation of doctors to things on high, and their humble descent for the sake of the weak to human things; in the amethyst, the continual memory of the heavenly kingdom in the mind of the humble. And each of the precious stones is assigned to a separate foundation. For although all the perfect, by whom the city of our God in His holy mountain is adorned and established, are refulgent with the light of spiritual grace, yet, "To one is given by the Spirit the word of wisdom; to another the word of knowledge by the same Spirit; to another faith in the same Spirit; to another the gifts of healing in the same Spirit; to another the working of miracles; to another prophecy; to another discerning of spirits; to another divers kinds of tongues; to another the interpretation of tongues." And God. "the builder and maker" of this city, Who is the foundation of foundations, and Who vouchsafed also to be made a High-Priest for us, that He might both cleanse and dedicate the walls of the same city by the offering of His blood, possesses all things as His own, "whatsoever the Father hath." Therefore, also, the same stones, inscribed too with the names of the twelve patriarchs, were commanded to be placed upon the breast of the high-priest, that in a most beautiful mystery it might be shewn that all the spiritual gifts which each of the saints individually and partially received, were equally and perfectly complete in "the mediator between God and man, the Man Jesus Christ."

This exposition of the precious stones I seem, perhaps, to have made more fully than the method of interpretation by clauses expressed. For it was necessary to explain carefully their qualities and their country, then to inquire into their sacramental meaning, and further to treat of their order and number. But as regards the profoundness of the subject itself, I seem to myself to have said very few things, and those briefly and summarily. And I suppliantly beseech the reader, if he shall perceive that I have trod in the right path, to give thanks to God; and if he shall discover that it has happened otherwise than as I desired, then to pray for pardon unto my error from the Lord. But these things so far: let us see also those which remain.

21. pearls. All the glory of the Head is imputed to the body. And as "the true light which lighteth every man," gave to the saints to be "the light of the world;" so also, although He Himself is the matchless pearl which the wise merchant sells all that he has to buy, He nevertheless compares His own with the brightness of pearls.

gold. He forms the streets of the same metals with which he had already said that the city was adorned For there are many, even of a commoner and lower life, who are surrounded with the highest virtues in the Church, and who shine with a purity of mind and an effulgence of work.

22. no temple. Although, he says, I have spoken of the city as built up of stones, I have shewn that the rest of the saints is not in a material building. For God Himself is their only home, and light, and rest.

23. no need. That is, because the Church is not guided by the light, nor the elements of the world, but is conducted by Christ, the eternal Sun, through the darkness of the world.

lighten. This is, we shall enjoy in that country the very light itself, by which we are now guided while we walk in the way; and being made blessed, we shall then perceive only that which is good, through the same by which we are now taught to discern between good and evil.

24. walk. He signifies that the same Lamb Himself is now to travellers the way, Who will then be to citizens the life.

kings. He here means spiritual kings, who bestow all the riches of their virtues upon the praises of the Church.

25. night. He relates that there will be the perpetual light of the Lamb; yea, rather that He Himself will be for an everlasting light in that city when the time of night is taken away. But that the gates will not be shut is a proof of the fullest security. For there it is no longer said, "Watch and pray, lest ye enter into temptation," but rather, "Be still then, and know that I am God."

26. bring. It is for this reason that it is to be gathered together from all nations.

27. enter. He describes the Church of that time, When, the bad having already been separated from the midst of it, the good alone will reign with Christ. But even now, too, every one who is unclean and false, is not in the Church, nor sees the light of the city of God, Who hateth him, "because the darkness has blinded his eyes."

ON CHAPTER 22

v. 1. river. In the river of life which flows in the midst of the city, there is no longer indicated the celebration of Baptism, but the fruit of that sacrament is now revealed. For in the present time the Church "sows in the Spirit, that it may then reap eternal life."

2. life. The tree of life is seen by the fountain of life; and whether thou interpret this to be the glory of the holy cross, or the Lord Christ, Who even before baptism was revealed already in the Old Testament, as He is now by the mystery of baptism becoming manifest, it alike endues the saints with heavenly fruit. For "Neither is there any other name under heaven given to men in which we must be saved;" seeing that the same tree which John described as flourishing in the golden Jerusalem and Moses in Paradise, Solomon pronounced to be "a tree of life to those who laid hold upon it." This I think to have been prefigured by the Jordan, on the other side of which Moses made known to the people the precepts of salvation, as Jesus on this side of it the land of promise.

month. In the twelve months he intimates all the time of life; the life, namely, in which it is said, "And thy years shall not fail;" and again, "It shall be month after month, and Sabbath after Sabbath;" where the face of the Lord is present, and is the eternal health, the eternal food of life. It may also be understood simply that the cross of Christ bears fruit through the doctrine of the twelve Apostles.

leaves. If the fruit is taken to be the reward of a blessed immortality, the leaves are rightly understood to be a perpetual song, in that it is for health to those who sing in their now blissful lot For there is the true healing of the nations, full redemption, everlasting bliss.

4. see. The vision of God is reserved to us as the reward of faith, and Philip understood this to be the chief good, when he said, "Lord, shew us the Father, and it sufficeth us." For it was diligently to be inculcated, that the saints would see and possess in reality that which they believe while living from faith.

name. The confession of the holy Name, which is now maintained in the midst of enemies, then in their own country makes glorious the conquerors.

5. night. There no frailness of the body needs either the repose of night or the light of fire, at the time in which God, Who is the true light, and the eternal rest of the saints, will be all in all. But if thou refer the words to an allegory, there no exhortation of the prophets, no preaching of the law, are necessary, which are now said to be "a lamp shining in a dark place;" seeing that in the contemplation of God all things are fulfilled, and the promise is possessed in its completeness.

6. faithful. He doubted not as to a want of faith in John. But he commended the truth of the vision to all the Church, in which he knew that there would also be little ones.

prophets. Doubt not, he says, of the person of him who shews. For God Himself, Who is wont to imbue the spirits of the prophets with heavenly vision, sent me to shew to thee beforehand that these things will be.

servants. He taught that the profit of all men generally has by him been foreseen.

7. book. "I am blessed," is understood. So the blessed Dionysius, Bishop of Alexandria, connects these clauses. For upon certain heresies arising on occasion of this book, he both refuted the error, and at the same time transferred to the eternal and heavenly promises the sense of the same prophecy, which he had purified from every cloud of carnal interpretation.

fell. He either did a second time that which had once been done, and which, when forbidden, he did not dare to repeat; or he is overwhelmed with amazement at the vision, and confesses that he again desires to worship.

9. fellowservant. Observe how often he both names John a prophet, and this book a prophecy. For he has many things in accordance with the prophets, and that not in sense alone, but also in words; for how many verses of Isaiah, how many of Zechariah, and of other prophets, wilt thou find here?

10. Seal. When the judgment which is to come draws near, it behoves the divine precepts, judgments, and promises to be manifested, by toe observation of which the meek are to obtain a reward, and through neglect of them the obstinate to incur punishment.

11. still. He here demonstrates the secret but just judgments of God, by which bad men are permitted to advance to something worse, that is, to arrive at the highest wickedness, that it may find a just judgment. Like to this is that, "Either make the tree good, and its fruit good, or make the tree bad, and its fruit bad."

13. Omega. In A he designates the divinity of the Word, and in Ω the humanity assumed, the beginning without end; which is confirmed by frequent repetition this book, either to intimate the divinity and humanity of the one Christ from time to time; or that the whole Trinity may be declared to be of one nature, Which saith by the prophet, "Before Me was there no God formed, neither shall there be after Me."

14. right. He promises a fit reward to "white robes," that is, an immaculate life, namely, that it may enjoy the sight of God, Who is eternal life. For, "Blessed are the pure in heart, for they shall see God."

enter. They who keep the commandments of the Lord, Who says, "I am the door; by Me if any man enter in he shall be saved, and shall go in and out, and find pasture," that assuredly which is here also promised of the tree of life; these without doubt enter in through the gates into the Church, the gates, namely, of righteousness, which the Psalmist desires to be opened unto himself. But he who endeavours "to climb up some other way, the same is a thief and a robber;" and of such also is added that which follows.

15. without. For all the madness of the wicked even now attack the Church from within. But when the "Master of the house shall have entered in, and as he saints enter with him unto the marriage," shall have closed the door, "then will they begin to stand without, and knock at the door."

16. David. Here he expressed the twofold nature of His person, namely, that the same was David's Maker, according to His divinity, Who "was made of the seed of David, according to the flesh." And this question the Lord proposes to the Jews in the Gospel, namely, how "Christ is the Son of David," when "David in the Spirit called Him Lord?"

star. For by appearing after the night of a single Passion, He shewed to the ages the light of resurrection and of life, by word and example. And of Him it is said to the blessed Job, "Dost thou bring forth Lucifer in his season?"

17. bride. The Head and the body of the Church exhort each one of the members to faith.

Come. Whosoever has received in his mind the inner light of faith, or of love, let him invite others also to this.

will. So far forth is free-will allowed by saying, "He who will, let him take;" that grace is set forth immediately in that which follows, "The water of life," with no merits assuredly preceding. For even to will is the gift of God.

18. add. These things he said on account of falsifiers, not on account of those who simply say what they think, without mutilating the prophecy in any respect.

20. testimony. The same Christ gives testimony, Who announces to the Church that He will come, to Whom after the manner of the Song of Songs the Church devoutly answers, "Amen; come, Lord Jesus Christ." And this she cries continually, saying, "Thy kingdom come;" and in the Psalm, "I will sing, and have understanding in the perfect way, when Thou shalt come unto me."

21. grace. Let the Pelagians, if they will, be confident in their own virtue, and deprive themselves of the grace of the Lord. But when the Apostle Paul seeks for help, and says, "Who shall deliver me from the body of this death," let John make answer, mindful of his own name, and say, "The grace of God, by Jesus Christ our Lord." And that the Donatists may not flatter themselves as having a singular gift of God, let them hear that when he imparted the grace of God, as a last farewell he added, "With you all. Amen."

And now that at length so great and hazardous a labour has been completed, I suppliantly and earnestly entreat, that if any shall think this little work of mine worth reading or transcribing, they will also remember to commend unto the Lord the author of the work, inasmuch as "I have not laboured for myself alone, but for them also." May I in return be rewarded by the vows and prayers of those who have the benefit of my toil; and may they, by their good offices, cause me to gain the right to and fruition of the tree of life, the odour and good report of which I have in some measure communicated to them.

Printed in Great Britain
by Amazon

40201557R00068